Cosmic Breadcrumbs

Cosmic Breadcrumbs

BUILDING A PROFITABLE PARTNERSHIP
WITH THE UNIVERSE

Joshua Dean Church

© 2025 by Joshua Dean Church
All rights reserved.

Without limiting the rights under copyright reserved above, no part of this publication may be reproduced, stored in or introduced into a retrieval system, or transmitted, in any form, or by any means (electronic, mechanical, photocopying, recording, or otherwise), without the prior permission of the copyright owner.

ISBN: 979-8-9937844-0-3

Book Design by Sarah Katreen Hoggatt, Book Layout Biz
Editorial Direction by Emily Sutherland
Creative Direction by Jacob Church, Rachel Church, Nina Barber, and Linda Church

Printed in the United States of America

CONTENTS

FOREWORD by Chad Sonkin ix

INTRODUCTION
The Finish Line xiii

PART I
The Seeker: An Inner Revolution

➤ **CHAPTER 1**
Three Thousand Miles From Home 3

➤ **CHAPTER 2**
One More Chance 13

➤ **CHAPTER 3**
The Fork in the Road 21

➤ **CHAPTER 4**
Training Camp 31

➤ **CHAPTER 5**
Bending The Rules 39

➤ **CHAPTER 6**
The Wine Opener 47

➤ **CHAPTER 7**
The Return 57

➤ **CHAPTER 8**
Ask and You Shall Receive 63

➤ **CHAPTER 9**
Find The Others 73

➤ **CHAPTER 10**
We'll See 79

➤ **CHAPTER 11**
The Call of The Edge 87

➤ **CHAPTER 12**
If I Really Loved Myself 99

PART II
The Builder: An Outer Experiment

➤ **CHAPTER 13**
The COVID Cousin Project 109

➤ **CHAPTER 14**
Going All In 115

➤ **CHAPTER 15**
Fifty Tubs and a Dream 125

➤ **CHAPTER 16**
With a Little Help from My Friends 135

➤ **CHAPTER 17**
From Castle to Kingdom 143

➤ **CHAPTER 18**
Order Up 151

➤ **CHAPTER 19**
The Growth You Asked For 161

➤ **CHAPTER 20**
Built For Winter 169

➤ **CHAPTER 21**
Setting the Temperature 177

➤ **CHAPTER 22**
Man in the Arena 183

➤ **CHAPTER 23**
This Is The Fun, You See 191

➤ **CHAPTER 24**
The Crucible Chronicles 201

➤ **CHAPTER 25**
The Next Breadcrumb 213

To my Mother and Father, for giving me The World.

Foreword by Chad Sonkin

PICTURE THIS.

You're sitting at home, minding your own business, when your best friend calls and says, "Hey, bro, will you write the foreword to my book?"

My first thought: *Wow, what an honor!* My second thought: *A foreword to your book? You want* me *to do what? I'm not even sure I've ever read a foreword.*

But when your best friend is Joshua Church, you don't overthink it—you just say *yes*. Because somehow, saying *yes* to Joshua always ends up changing my life.

Our friendship started as two kids living in the basement of a fraternity house in the cornfields of Ohio. (Yes, you'll read that story soon). From day one, we bonded over dreams and purpose. We both felt it: that we were here for a reason and that we were writing our own story. We wanted to live fully, intentionally—to dream big and go all in. With our crew, it felt like nothing was impossible.

And Joshua has always led the way.

One night, I gave a speech to rally our fraternity, which was on the verge of getting kicked off campus. Afterward, Joshua pulled me aside.

"Bro, did you notice that?" he said.

"Notice what?"

"When you speak, everyone listens. You inspired them with your energy. That's a real gift you have, and part of what you are here to share."

That moment hit me hard and opened up a whole new possibility for my life. No friend had ever seen me like that before. It reminded me of a quote from Clementine Churchill:

> "After dining with Mr. Gladstone, I thought he was the cleverest man in England. After dining with Mr. Disraeli, I thought *I* was the cleverest woman in England."

That's Joshua. After one conversation with him, you feel like the smartest, bravest, or most capable version of yourself. He has this way of seeing people that lifts them higher—of reminding people who they really are. I've felt it countless times, and I've seen him do it with everyone from lifelong friends to Uber drivers.

And now, it's your turn. Somehow, through these pages, he's managed to see *you*—and left breadcrumbs for you to find the truths you've always hoped were real to open up a new possibility for your life.

Though I call Joshua my best friend, I've also called him roommate, brother, co-worker, asshole (on the basketball court—he's a competitor lol), and even boss. Yes, he was my boss. Together, we recruited and led a team that built a $20 million company in three years, which you'll read about in this journey.

I've seen Joshua under pressure, behind closed doors, and deep in the trenches of his own growth—mental, physical, and spiritual. He doesn't just talk the talk. He walks it. Trust me when I say that every lesson he shares in this book has been embodied on the deepest of levels. And with this book, he opens his heart and invites you in with a level of honesty that takes real courage.

Now, let's get something straight—this isn't your typical "self-help" book. Matter of fact, I don't even know what "self-help" is supposed to mean.

This is a *self-first* book. It's for those ready to finally put themselves first—not out of ego, but out of love. Because, as Joshua always reminds me, it's not about you; it's for the people you love. The ones who depend on your clarity, your strength, and your light. That's why we have to show up for ourselves first.

Inside these pages, you'll find the foundation for the real work—the work of dreaming relentlessly, of showing up fully awake, of learning to ride life's waves through the highs and the lows, allowing the current to pull you forward. As J. Cole says, "If you want to tap into your greatness, this is the starter kit." That's what this book is: your starter kit. A manual for aligning with the Universe instead of fighting against it. A roadmap for living with your head up, heart open, and eyes wide.

It's about trusting what you can't yet see, turning setbacks into strength, and—most importantly—having fun now. It's about playing the infinite game for joy, no matter what the scoreboard says.

So dog-ear these pages, highlight the hell out of them, and come back to this story whenever you forget who you are—and again when you remember.

Because this isn't just a book you read; it's a book you *do*. It's a mirror, a reminder, a cosmic nudge back to yourself. It will challenge you, comfort you, and call you higher. Take a breath, open your heart, and let Joshua guide you through what only he could write.

I am low-key jealous that you get to experience this for the first time. All I can say is, buckle up.

Introduction

The Finish Line

MILE 139. Fifteen hours and forty-nine minutes in. One mile to go.

My headlamp cuts through the darkness of the Arizona night, its narrow beam illuminating just enough of the cold pavement to guide my next few steps. I jog forward slowly. The rhythm of my exhales blending with the soft thud of my feet pacifies my mind as if it were a lullaby. Every time my right foot lands, I feel the faint squish of something inside my sock. Blood from a blister, I realize, but that's a tomorrow problem.

I'm in deep. The kind of deep where pain becomes a companion instead of an enemy. Hours ago, my body screamed with protest, but now I've reached a strange state of flow—gliding forward like a slow, determined zombie. I see the infamous Mile Marker 25 of the marathon portion of the race. One mile to go.

I attempt to pick up my pace, only to be greeted by a sharp, stabbing pain in my knee. The same pain that forced me to walk the entirety of Mile 15. I stop for a moment, placing my hands on my hips and taking a long, deliberate exhale. "You're okay," I say softly to my body, like soothing a child. "I got you. I love you. We're almost there."

The pain subsides. I keep going.

I glance at my watch: 11:32 p.m. I can't remember the last time I stayed up this late. Jumping into the water for the 2.6-mile swim at 7:00 a.m. feels like a lifetime ago. Battling gusting headwinds during the 112-mile bike ride is a blur, like a distant memory that belongs to someone else.

And then, without warning, a wave of unexpected emotion crashes over me: laughter. It starts small, a chuckle born from sheer exhaustion, but soon it grows into full-on, almost maniacal laughter. I'm laughing at the absurdity of it all. *What the hell am I doing? How did I end up here, on a quiet November night in Tempe, Arizona, about to cross the finish line of a full Ironman Triathlon?*

I think about the lost, scared, broken kid I once was. I think about the doctor who told that seventeen-year-old to "pick up golf" because I was too injury-prone for anything more. I think about the emergency surgery that almost cost me my leg and the grueling recovery that followed. And the feeling of my first blood transfusion when I was clinging to life itself. I think about the overwhelming sense of limbo I lived in, feeling lost in my career, unsure of what I was doing or where I was headed, or what I even wanted to do with my life. I remember the weight of deep depression, moving through the days like a stranger trapped in my own body while living in chronic pain.

The sound of cheering fans in the distance brings my focus back to the task at hand. The music is louder now, and I can see the lights from the finish line up ahead. I see the red carpet straightaway, which instantly sends chills buzzing down my spine one vertebrae at a time. The same red carpet I was denied years before, when I had to pull out of my first attempt at the Ironman. A hit of adrenaline and a surge of dopamine numbs any remaining pain in my heavy legs.

I hit the red carpet and feel like I'm floating, weightless, in a moment that feels both surreal and eternal. My arms stretch wide, my head tilts back, and a smile overtakes me—a smile born from sheer gratitude and disbelief. To my right, I see my friends and family crowded by the finish line chute, cheering wildly, their joy overflowing and contagious. That sight shatters me open, and a wave of raw emotion overtakes me like a flood I can't hold back. Tears stream down my face, carving paths through layers of sunscreen, dried sweat, and desert dust. Each tear feels like a river, returning home to the cracked, thirsty earth below.

"Joshua Church!" the announcer's voice booms over the speaker. "We see the gratitude, Joshua—you are an Ironman!" Sparklers erupt above the finish line as I step across it, into a moment I know I will carry with me for the rest of my life.

My cousin, Rob, is standing just past the finish line, waiting for me with open arms. He finished a few minutes ahead of me and is there to receive me. We're both crying uncontrollably when he wraps me in an embrace. Rob and I have crossed many finish lines together before, but this one is different. This was the first *full* Ironman together, and we did it wearing our Edge Theory Labs race uniforms—a company we had built together from scratch just two years earlier. We limp toward the crowd of friends, family, and teammates waiting on the other side, and the magnitude of what we've accomplished begins to settle in.

Cat, one of my closest friends and our Director of Marketing, flings her arms around me, buzzing with excitement. Her eyes sparkle as if she's been holding back a firework all day, waiting for the perfect moment to let it explode. Chad, my best friend and our Director of Sales, steps in right after her, pulling me into a bear hug. His hand thumps my arm, solid and reassuring, like he's trying to ground me before the weight of the news hits—news I didn't yet know but was about to find out. His grin is impossibly wide, radiating so much joy it feels contagious.

"We did $158,000 in sales today while you were racing!" Cat bursts out, her voice cracking with exhilaration.

Standing there, surrounded by my people, I felt like I had arrived at the intersection of everything I had worked for and everything I had once only dreamed was possible. I had a business that was making millions of dollars a month, friends and teammates I loved, and a connection to my body that carried me across the finish line of one of the most grueling endurance races on Earth.

I step aside to have a moment to myself, admiring the fanfare of the finish line. I hadn't planned any of this. I couldn't have. Sure, there were goals, training schedules, and business meetings along the way. But standing there, I knew this moment hadn't come from strategy alone. It had come from something wilder and deeper, something I couldn't fully explain at the time.

That November in 2023, we would surpass $2 million in sales, more than we had done in all of 2022, our first year of business. And if that weren't surreal enough, just a few days later, I would check off another lifelong dream: being named to the Forbes 30 Under 30 list. That Forbes logo had occupied my vision board throughout my twenties, right next to a photo of an Ironman finish line.

I thought back to the punch-drunk question I posed at Mile 25: *How the hell did I get here?* Now I knew. I hadn't followed a plan.

I followed the cosmic breadcrumbs.

Those quiet whispers and subtle nudges. The synchronicities and winks from the Universe. The detours that end up being direction. The cosmic clues littered along my path like a yellow brick road. The path never made sense while I was on it—but now, looking back, I could see the thread. The signs were always there. I just had to learn how to listen.

In a world that glorifies certainty and control, where success is measured by five-year plans and carefully curated timelines, we're taught to believe that we alone must have it all figured out. That being self-made is the highest badge of honor. That deviation from the plan will surely mean failure. No wonder so many of us feel stuck, burnt out, or quietly lost—following paths that look good on paper but feel hollow in the soul.

But what if there's another way?

What if the goal was never to *figure it all out*...but to learn how to listen? What if life wasn't meant to be controlled, but *collaborated with*—a creative force that's been trying to get your attention all along?

It is clear to scientists, skeptics, and believers alike that there is an intelligent, creative force present—call it God, the Universe, Source, Spirit, Science, Life. It's the same force that governs gravity and pulls the tides. The force that fuels the burning stars and has programmed the miracle of photosynthesis within the plant kingdom. It's the force that keeps us breathing without effort, even while we sleep, and turns the caterpillar into a butterfly. We can all agree that this force is present and abundant. So what if maybe, *just maybe*, that same creative, intelligent force is available to you as well?

To follow the cosmic breadcrumbs is to build a *partnership* with that force in a co-creative relationship. It's about daring to believe that this force is actually on your side. That it is quietly (and sometimes not so quietly) conspiring on your behalf, dropping clues and signs to help you remember who you are. That it's guiding you towards what you truly desire on the path of least resistance. Following cosmic breadcrumbs is about recognizing that this force is always speaking to you, through a quiet whisper of your intuition, leaving one breadcrumb at a time, revealing your next step.

Each breadcrumb along the way is sacred. Not just the glittering ones wrapped in ease and beauty, but the messy, painful ones too. The ones that arrive disguised as lumps of coal: the losses, the heartbreaks, the moments that bring you to your knees. Choosing to follow the cosmic breadcrumbs means sitting with these, too, and honoring them as the teachers they are. Trusting they're part of the process. Staying with them long enough—through the pressure and heat—to witness the transformation they bring. To watch life's creative force turn even the darkest breadcrumb into something luminous—into the diamond it was always meant to become.

This path has carried me to adventures I never could have dreamed of. It has brought me to my knees, taught me how to heal, and revealed a passion and purpose I didn't know I had. Not only did this path lead me to my calling in life, it guided me step-by-step to turn it into a $20 million business in less than three years. The truth is, I never had it all figured out. I just kept following the next cosmic breadcrumb.

Because somehow, at every turn, a sign would appear to guide me. At every obstacle, a ladder was hidden in the bushes, waiting to be discovered. In moments of challenge, support would arrive, and whenever I was most in need, the right teacher would appear. Time and again, when I felt like there was no way forward, a miracle would unfold. And after each battle I fought, each curveball life threw my way, I could look back with clarity, seeing the hidden gifts those moments carried—each one ultimately leading me closer to what I had been seeking all along.

Crossing that finish line was a peak experience, a culmination of years of grit and dreams brought to life. It was one of those rare moments I wish I could pause forever. But life doesn't let us linger at the peaks. Less than one year after the high of that finish line, we would have to make a series of impossible choices and lose millions of dollars. I would wrestle with an identity crisis that forced me to confront fears I thought I'd conquered long ago.

Still, the breadcrumbs kept showing up. Sometimes they were right in front of me. Other times, I had to dig for them. But they were always there, quietly guiding me forward. That's the thing. The Universe is the only partnership that guarantees a return. You might lose money, people, a business, or plans, but you'll always profit in wisdom, alignment, clarity, and peace.

This book is an invitation to begin following your own trail of cosmic breadcrumbs. To build a deeper trust with your intuition and strengthen that muscle. To embrace the mystery, lean into the unknown, and establish a partnership with the Universe and a relationship with this higher power. To dare to dream out loud and find the others who also choose to live in this way. It's a call to live with more wonder, more curiosity, with more aliveness. A reminder that your path isn't something you have to force—it's something you can follow. And that the answers to your greatest questions are always within reach.

I've chosen to break this book into two natural parts because they need each other. You can't have one without the other.

The first part, **The Seeker: An Inner Revolution**, is about the journey that started long before any business did. It's the story of finding my path, discovering my gifts, and learning the language of the Universe's subtle winks, nudges, and whispers—the breadcrumbs that led me home to myself. It's about the healing, the unlearning, and the building of the internal foundation first.

The second part, **The Builder: An Outer Experiment**, is where all of that inner work gets tested in the real world. It's the story of Edge Theory Labs, the company I co-founded, that reveals what becomes possible when you build from a place of alignment. It's about the magic and the mess of bringing spiritual principles into business—how creation becomes its own form of initiation, and how sometimes, the experiment has to fall apart to reveal a more profound truth.

Together, these two parts form one whole story: the inner revolution that made the outer experiment possible—and the outer experiment that deepened the inner revolution.

As you move through these pages, you'll see references to the books, songs, films, quotes, and talks that helped shape me. Each one played a role in the curriculum of becoming, of building this foundation. I've gathered all of these resources into a living, ever-growing list. You can access it for free by scanning the QR code in the book where you will also find another invitation.

Wherever you are in your journey, let this story—the triumphs, the trials, the tribulations, and everything in between—be a mirror for your own. A permission slip to slow down, pay attention, and listen for the subtle signs. Because life *is* leaving you clues. It's speaking to you in riddles and rhymes, daring you to pay attention.

If you've picked up this book, maybe your next breadcrumb is waiting in these pages.

Are you ready?

Part I

The Seeker: An Inner Revolution

CHAPTER 1

Three Thousand Miles From Home

"You're from San Diego, why are you here?"

A condescending voice boomed from the row behind me in Microbiology 111 on the first day of my freshman year of college.

The lecture hall was filled with a couple hundred people, and I turned back to greet the preppy kid with a comb-over haircut who was glaring at me seriously.

I was beginning to ask myself the same question. Three thousand miles from home, from comfort, from everything I knew, I wondered what I was doing in the cornfields of small-town Oxford, Ohio attending Miami University.

I wanted to say, "The same reason you are here, buddy." It was only the first day of school, but I was already used to fielding shocked faces when people learned that I was from San Diego, California. Most of them had never been to California, evident in the way they called it "Cali" and asked me if I surfed, smoked weed, and knew anyone famous. And I guess since my answer was *yes* to all three questions, I wasn't exactly breaking the stereotype.

I replied, "Well, my grandparents went to school here, and I used to live in Cleveland when I was younger, so a bunch of cousins and family friends went here and all loved it. I visited and decided to come here."

That seemed to satisfy his initial concern. Though he still seemed a bit puzzled, he introduced himself.

"I'm Ryland Puzzitiello, he said."

"I'm Joshua. Nice to meet you."

It's funny how the trail of cosmic breadcrumbs works. On that late-August morning in 2013, if you had told me all that the next eight years would hold for Ryland and me, I would have given you the same puzzled look he gave me that day.

Ryland and I didn't become instant friends. We were classmates who occasionally texted in the same group chat with a few others from class, asking about due dates and assignments. This first class was an indication of how my first semester went. I felt like an outsider. I came to campus not knowing a single person, and I was adjusting to a whole new culture. My Volcom shorts and high white Nike socks reaching up from my Vans stuck out like a sore thumb amidst Vineyard Vines whales and freshly oiled Sperrys. I ate lunch and meals alone, spending most of my time in my dorm binge-watching TV shows and talking on the phone to my friends from home. I walked around campus with my head down and headphones on.

This was all a drastic contrast to my life back in San Diego, where I graduated from a small 120-person class with kids I'd known since elementary school. I left high school feeling like a big fish in a small pond. I was student body president, captain of the football and basketball teams, and had great relationships with my teachers and deans, who allowed me to come and go from class as I pleased. Now, I wasn't just a small fish in a big pond; I was a fish caught in a tree branch, trying to ask the birds for directions to the nearest body of water. I felt every one of those 3,000 miles between me and home.

I was enrolled in the business school, telling myself I was on the right path, even though I had no idea what that path actually looked like. I just knew I wanted to do something great with my life, something that mattered. There was this restless feeling under the surface, that I was meant for more, but I couldn't yet name what "more" was. I wanted to believe I could create something spectacular, something that felt true to me, but I was lost in the noise of expectations and uncertainty. I just didn't want life to pass me by. I felt a quiet ache of possibility without a clear direction, an inner tug. As those first few weeks unfolded, I somehow wasn't sure if I would, in fact, find my path on this college campus.

There were distractions and adjustments that took the front seat. My drinking, partying, and eating habits quickly added the freshman fifteen, and above all, my body became inflamed and unwell. My face swelled, I had a beer belly. Muscles atrophied away from my chest and arms. It all escalated to a crescendo one evening in early November.

On a bone-chilling Ohio night familiar to few, I found myself doubled over with stomach pain in my dorm room. A bottle of Pepto-Bismol and a roll of Tums later, I was still in excruciating pain. I called Mom and she told me to go to the hospital. She was worried that it could be appendicitis. I was about a mile and a half away from the hospital and was in no condition to walk. I felt embarrassed to knock on the door of the only kid in our hall who had a car, who I only kind of knew, to ask for a ride to the hospital. But at this point, embarrassment and loneliness were feelings I had become used to.

As if I needed another reason to believe that *Mom always knows*, she did.

The scan confirmed it: appendicitis. The doctor said my appendix needed to be removed right away before it burst. I called my parents to explain everything, doing my best to sound casual.

"Hey Mom, just a minor hiccup," I said. "The scans confirmed it is appendicitis. They're taking it out tonight. Totally routine. I'll be back in my dorm tomorrow and in class the next day. You really don't need to fly out."

There was a pause on the line. Her voice was measured, but full of concern. "Joshua, are you sure? I really think I should be there."

"Seriously, I'm fine," I said, trying to sound convincing. "It's not worth the trip. I got this."

She hesitated, then finally gave in. "Okay. But please keep me updated, every step."

"Promise," I said.

We hung up just as the nurse came over to prep me for surgery. I breathed in as deeply as I could before the pain shot up again, feeling proud I'd handled it all on my own.

Or so I thought.

I lay in the hospital bed in the late hours of the night, waiting to be wheeled into the operating room, feeling completely alone. The cold air clung to my skin, and the harsh fluorescent lights made the room feel more like an interrogation chamber than a place of healing. It wasn't my first time in a hospital, and the sterile smells and distant echoes pulled me back to memories I thought I'd buried. The only flickers of comfort came from golf playing softly on a faraway TV and the rhythmic shuffle of solitaire cards from the nurse's computer.

As I waited, an old, familiar thought slipped into the projector room of my mind and began playing on a loop. *You're broken!* The words didn't just appear—they arrived like the spectacle of an opening title screen, with trumpets, lights, and fanfare. I felt like those words weren't just introducing the movie of my life. They were producing it, directing it, shaping every scene. My stomach dropped. I thought I ditched this old story back in San Diego, yet here it was chasing me no matter how many miles I ran.

On the screen in my mind, the film kept rolling. Scene after scene unfolding—moments I hadn't revisited in years. And just like that, I was back at the beginning.

"We're not sure about the extent of the brain damage."

Those were the first words my mother heard after I was born. After 26 hours of labor and an emergency C-section, I came into the world with a collapsed lung and a cone-shaped head, immediately hooked up to wires and tubes in the NICU. Mom didn't get to hold me for five days. Maybe that rocky beginning foreshadowed what was to come.

As a kid, my energy couldn't be contained. Some kids bounce off the walls—I bounced *into* them. My parents used to call me "Josh of the Jungle," half in awe, half in warning. I'd leap off couches in my homemade loincloth, howling mid-air, usually ending with a crash and a bruise. Casts, crutches, and ER visits became a regular part of my life.

By ten, I was on a first-name basis with the orthopedic tech, Chuck. After yet another injury—this time a broken elbow—my dad turned to the doctor and asked, "Why do you think he keeps getting hurt? Maybe he has a calcium deficiency or brittle bones?"

It was a simple question, asked out of the most beautiful intentions of love and concern. But what I heard in my ten-year-old brain was something entirely different:

I must be broken.

That single sentence hacked its way into the source code of my very operating system and grew into the belief that my body was faulty, that something was fundamentally wrong with me. *Why did my body keep failing me?*

After all, that belief had been lurking since the very first breath I took. *Maybe there is something wrong with me.* I didn't say it out loud back then, but it had been growing quietly inside me like a weed. Rooting deeper every year. Shaping how I saw myself. Shaping what I thought I was capable of.

And over time, life gave me plenty of evidence to prove it right.

At sixteen, I tore my ACL, MCL, LCL, and meniscus in a brutal football injury. I needed a full knee reconstruction and had to relearn how to walk. The following year, at seventeen, I came within hours of having my right leg amputated after I was diagnosed with Compartment Syndrome—a rare acute condition where internal swelling cuts off blood flow to the rest of the limb. At eighteen, it was a herniated disc followed by chronic back pain. I groaned like an old man jumping down from the ledge my friends and I ate lunch on in high school. And so, at nineteen, finding myself in a hospital bed once again—for the fourth year in a row—somehow wasn't surprising anymore. It was starting to feel like a pattern I couldn't avoid and an event as consistent as my birthday.

At the time, I couldn't see these injuries for what they were. I hadn't yet learned that the body has its own language. That pain is a message, and symptoms are signals—whispers asking for attention. And when whispers go unheard, they get louder until they become shouts. I couldn't yet see those injuries as breadcrumbs waiting for me.

"You ready?" The nurse abruptly interrupts my thoughts while unlocking the hospital bed's wheels to roll me to the operating room.

"Ready as I'll ever be." I quip back with a smile.

At least, unlike my past injuries, I felt some relief in knowing that this was a routine surgery and that I would be back in action tomorrow.

The first snowfall of the year drifted through the town, soft and silent, as I lay under the knife in a sterile operating room. When I woke up after surgery, the room was spinning. My mouth tasted of metal and anesthesia. I drifted in and out of consciousness, waking only to vomit into a plastic basin as the nurses swapped it out again and again. The fluorescent lights felt like they were burning through my eyelids. Every sound, from the steady beep of the monitor to the shuffle of rubber soles in the hallway, echoed through my skull. My cousin Isaac drove hours to be with me, his short visit passing in a haze I could barely hold onto.

Something was off. I could feel it in my bones, in the way my body refused to calm.

Hours later, when a nurse cheerfully told me it was time to be discharged, I could barely lift my head. My vision blurred, the edges of the room folded in and out of focus. "Are you sure I'm able to go?" I managed, my voice raw and small. "I still don't feel right."

She smiled the kind of smile meant to reassure but not to listen. "Totally normal," she said. "It's just the meds wearing off."

But deep down, I knew it wasn't.

They helped me to the side of the bed to stand, and the next thing I knew, I was waking up on the floor surrounded by nurses. I had passed out. When I tried to stand again, the same thing happened—this time I woke up in the hospital bed with a warm sensation spreading down my legs. I saw the worry spread over the nurses' faces as they finally believed me. The doctor decided to keep me longer and run tests.

I reached for my phone by the bedside, its screen blinking at 2%, and called Mom, desperate.

She answered on the second ring. Before I could speak, she said, "I'm just parking now, sweetie. I'll be up in five minutes."

Unbeknownst to me, her Jewish mother's instincts had already kicked in. She hadn't listened when I told her not to come; instead, she'd booked the first flight to Cincinnati.

For a moment, I wondered if I was hallucinating, if I'd misheard her and heard what I *hoped* she said. But then, in what felt like a blink, she appeared in the doorway. A wave of primal relief rushed through me in a way I had never experienced. Up to that point, I had only understood the concept of gratitude as a word. In that moment, as she walked toward my hospital bed, gratitude became a visceral feeling. She took one look at me, and I could see it in her eyes: Mama Bear had arrived.

The tests and scans confirmed that I was bleeding internally. The surgeon had accidentally nicked a blood vessel during the procedure, but we didn't learn that right away. All we could do was monitor my blood count closely and pray I wouldn't need to be taken back into surgery. I made it through the night, but there was no real improvement. I could feel the life in me thinning, draining away slowly, as if I was teetering on the edge of something, straddling between the longing to hold on and let go. The space between life and death felt frighteningly thin, almost like a doorway I could choose to walk through.

By morning, the doctors decided I needed a blood transfusion. A nurse came in and hung the bag above me. It was wrapped to conceal the contents, but they couldn't cover the tube. I watched the dark velvet red crawl its way slowly down the line. Then it entered my arm. I felt it instantly—a flush of warmth spread from the injection site, washing through my body like a heatwave of life.

Over the next four days in the hospital, I received multiple transfusions to rebuild my blood count. Slowly, I began to stabilize. My numbers started to rise. I was turning a corner and wouldn't need to go back into surgery.

Once discharged, I stayed in a nearby hotel with Mom for a week while I recovered, waiting for the doctor to give us the all-clear to fly. With at least a month of healing ahead, it was clear I wouldn't be returning to campus this semester. When we drove away from the school, just a couple of weeks before Thanksgiving break, I looked out at the red brick buildings and thought this was the last time I would ever set foot here.

Maybe there was nothing more for me in Ohio; perhaps it just wasn't meant to be.

Back home in San Diego, bedridden, things didn't get any easier. Darkness came in waves, and I was sinking fast. I was barely able to move, and to top it all off, I contracted pneumonia.

One night, a violent coughing fit rips me from sleep.

Each cough is a spark catching fire in my chest. I double over, clutching my side as pain rips through the stitches of my incision. The coughing builds until nausea takes over. Too weak to stand, dazed from a cocktail of pain meds, I roll off the bed and start crawling—literally crawling—toward the bathroom. My body feels like it's unraveling, thread by thread. By the time I reach the toilet, the coughing finally subsides just long enough for the vomiting to begin.

When it's over, I wipe my face and catch a glimpse of myself in the mirror. I grip the cold granite counter and pull myself upright, locking eyes with the stranger staring back. Tears pour from my hollow eyes. This isn't just a reflection; it's a confrontation.

I'm nineteen. Fresh off another surgery. And I feel completely broken. My body is frail, trembling, stitched together like a patchwork of pain. The loop in my head won't stop: *Why is this happening? How much more can I take? What did I do to deserve this?*

I'm angry. Defeated. I feel like I've been handed a lemon of a body—no warranty, no return policy—and forced to make do. I wear a smile for friends and family, but inside, I'm sinking. Depression has its claws in me. I'm exhausted. Tired of hurting. Tired of being tired. I started to believe this was it. That this was just how my life would be, and if this was it, was life even worth continuing?

That thought hangs between me and my reflection, heavy in the air like dark, thick smoke that is impossible to breathe through. For the first time, I speak to whatever or whoever might be listening, not out of faith but out of desperation.

If there's a reason I should still be here, I whisper between shaky breaths, *show me. Give me a sign. Please.*

The room holds its breath with me. Then, a small but certain pulse of light breaks the darkness.

The countertop nightlight flickers on, as if the Universe is answering, *I've got you.*

CHAPTER 2

One More Chance

"Exhale. Savasana."

My body surrendered, melting into the mat. Sweat streamed from my brow and pooled beneath me, a shimmering outline tracing where I'd fought and fallen, like a chalk silhouette at the scene of some quiet internal crime.

And then… stillness.

Whoa. Stillness. What a strange, foreign sensation.

After my doctor finally cleared me to move again, my Uncle David practically dragged me to this yoga class. He wasn't taking no for an answer, though I gave him plenty of reasons.

"Yoga? Like the girls do? No way," I'd said.

He just smirked. "Come to one class. If you hate it, you never have to come again."

Uncle David had made dramatic lifestyle changes and dropped forty-four pounds in what felt like the blink of an eye. He became proof of what's possible—a living reminder that change is possible, and no diagnosis is permanent. Watching his mind and body transform was enough evidence for me to give in to his request to try a hot sculpt yoga class. Maybe I could change, too. So I yielded, reluctantly and grudgingly, but somewhere beneath that resistance, a small and curious part of me hoped that this experience would be different.

Lying on the mat at the end of class, I felt a calm I'd never known before. My body, usually tight and screaming, was still. Relaxed, even. In that quietness, as I traced beads of sweat joining the reflective puddle around me, something unexpected happened. I heard a voice. Not the usual swirl of my own thoughts, but something clearer and quieter came through. *More of this*, it said. Only it didn't feel like a thought. It felt like a whisper from a deeper place, as if my body—or some part of me I hadn't known how to hear—was finally speaking up. Maybe it was the same voice that came to me that night in the bathroom mirror. That first yoga class didn't fix anything, but it gave me a moment of relief. Just enough to feel a tiny shift, and with it, a flicker of hope.

While I was home recovering during that winter break, I didn't miss a single yoga class for two and a half months. Every day, I showed up, now brave enough to try other styles of yoga. Slowly, things began to change in my body. Real, physical changes. I could sit on my knees again—something I thought would never happen after my knee surgery. I'd believed that range of motion was gone for good. That one small win pushed me to keep going and opened a new question: if my body could change, what else might be possible?

January rolled around, and I started looking into the option of transferring to a school closer to home. It seemed practical. With my health challenges, it made sense to stay near family, to keep this new rhythm, to be where I felt safe and steady.

I'd tried the Ohio thing. It didn't feel like me. But when I went to hit "submit" on the transfer application, I paused. That same inner voice returned—quiet, but certain. *Give it one more chance.* I didn't know why, but I listened.

More curious than convinced, I decided to go back for one more semester just to see. If it still didn't feel right, I could leave knowing I'd given it everything. So I packed my bags, said goodbye to my family, and got on the plane with cautious optimism—not sure where it would lead, but open enough to find out.

When I arrived, the ground was hard-packed with snow and the streets glazed with ice. I hurried from the taxi to my dorm, cranked the heat, and immediately started second-guessing my decision. My SoCal sun-kissed skin was no match for the icy gray Ohio sky and frozen sidewalks.

I'd come back early to make up a Calculus final I'd missed, one I needed a B on to pass the class. I met with my professor, took the test, and struggled through it mightily despite steady preparation throughout winter break. As I turned it in, my doubts deepened.

After the test, I turned my phone back on and saw a message from a student named Claffy.

"Party at Stonehouse, 10 p.m. Come through. Don't be an idiot, come."

Claffy was a junior and the recruitment chair for Sigma Phi Epsilon Fraternity. Built like a hockey player, always grinning, he had a raspy voice and a laugh that could cut through the blaring music of any party. He was the kind of guy who, after one conversation, would have an inside joke with you that made you feel special. It was a superpower.

I had met him through one of his roommates, a fellow San Diegan I was introduced to over the summer. They'd invited me to parties during first semester, but I usually passed, totally unaware that most guys were trying to get noticed for spring rush. I didn't know Claffy was the gatekeeper everyone was trying to impress—I was oblivious, which somehow worked in my favor.

So, freshly back on campus and determined to give it my all before transferring home, I say *yes*.

I arrive at the front steps of the fraternity annex house, a grand stone mansion looming like a medieval castle and aptly named *Stonehouse*. With its turrets and arched windows, it could have been plucked from a fairytale and dropped here as the ultimate fraternity party house. Music spills out the doorway as partiers crowd the patio and second-floor balcony.

Squeezing through the packed entrance, I'm swallowed by a sea of bodies, laughter, and heavy bass thumping through the floorboards. The air is thick with body heat and the sticky scent of beer, which is a strangely welcome change from the icy night outside. Voices rise over the music, bottles clink, and everyone is buzzing with excitement about being back on campus for second semester.

I reach the kitchen and grab a can of warm Natty Lite. Just as I crack it open, Claffy spots me and lights up.

"Church! You made it. Welcome back, you son of a bitch, I was almost worried you weren't gonna show."

Wrapping his thick, trunk-like forearms around me, he gives me the kind of rough hug an older brother gives a younger one, even though I'm five inches taller.

He then pulls me aside and leans in, all business. "Dude, glad you made it back."

He pauses, almost rehearsed. "On behalf of Sigma Phi Epsilon, we want to offer you an early bid to join the fraternity. How's that sound?"

He smiles, waiting.

It's an easy yes. I like the guys I've met; they're grounded, athletic, and fun. They work hard and play harder. Maybe this is my chance to make real friends. Maybe I can finally belong here.

"That sounds freaking great. I'm in!" I shout.

Claffy grins widely, throws an arm around me, and pulls me toward the crowd. "We got Church!" he yells, and the room erupts. Cheers, laughter, hugs. Strangers dap me up, hand me drinks, and introduce me to girls who flirtatiously kiss my cheek. After months of feeling like a ghost—invisible, uncertain, on the outside looking in—I finally feel seen.

Later, I hurry back to my dorm, careful not to slip on black ice, which is a new skill I never thought I'd need. My phone buzzes. An email from my Calculus professor lights up the screen: 83 on the final. I pass.

Relief floods through me. A wink from the Universe. It's confirmation that giving Ohio one more shot was not in vain, and yet another reason to continue to get to know and trust that voice inside me.

If the first semester was a biting cold Ohio winter, emotionally, the second semester was a San Diego summer beach day by contrast. Rather than going through my days without seeing or knowing any friends, eating meals alone with headphones in, I was instantly connected with one hundred guys within the fraternity and an entire Greek Life community of hundreds more. The campus suddenly felt a lot smaller and more accessible. I quickly became close with the thirty-five guys in our pledge class.

The only kid I recognized in our pledge class was none other than Ryland Puzzitiello, the serious kid who gave me that lovely greeting on our first day of classes in Microbiology 111. He seemed shocked that I made it into this fraternity. Though we hadn't been friends before, we were suddenly on the same team, even if we kept each other at arm's length.

At one of our first gatherings as a pledge class, I spotted a guy standing by the couch wearing a Star of David necklace. Meeting someone Jewish in that setting felt even rarer than meeting someone from San Diego. I made a beeline for him.

Up close, I noticed his bright auburn-red hair and a grin that stretched across his whole face. His presence made the room feel warmer, and when he smiled, his whole body seemed to smile with him, like his joy was too big to stay contained. He was built like the all-state football player he was—short and stocky, with thick biceps that made every shirt look one size too small. And his energy was huge. Not in a loud, overbearing way, just...*big*—like he was always on the edge of bouncing out of his own skin.

"No way—you're Jewish? Me too!" I said, grinning.

"Dude, no way that's amazing, let's fucking go! I'm Chad from Cleveland."

"I'm Josh from California."

"Cali?! No way, dude, that's so cool, I've always wanted to go there. Maybe one day," he said, eyes lighting up with genuine excitement.

We bonded immediately.

The third character I met was Danny Herrle. Danny jumped out to me as being the coolest kid in our pledge class. Not in a flashy way, but with a laid-back confidence that drew people in. He'd show up early to help set up for a party and stay late to clean up the mess. A loyal friend, a solid athlete, a sharp dresser, who somehow even pulled off diamond stud earrings that would've looked try-hard on anyone else. And behind that easy confidence, there was a stillness in his eyes, like he knew more than he let on. That was a depth about him that most people missed, which caught my attention. So we started hanging out, and pretty quickly, we became good friends.

As the semester went on, I discovered a whole new world—and culture—at college in Ohio. A few upperclassmen who lived at Stonehouse took a liking to me, which was essential for surviving pledging. They were always playing this card game called Euchre, which looked impossibly complicated, was played in teams of two, and had no logical rules. As they huddled on mismatched, sagging couches, after clearing bongs and two-day-old fast food bags off the coffee table, I sat back and watched.

Every day after class, before any pledging events, I headed to Stonehouse to observe. I studied the rituals of fraternity life: the drama, the hierarchies, the strategies, and the stories. I felt a bit like Nick Carraway in *The Great Gatsby*, watching it all unfold from just outside the circle—curious, slightly stunned, and a little high. The older guys talked about switching majors, summer internships, and how to game the job market with the least effort possible. Someone read his cover letter aloud like performance art while another ranted about drone surveillance and microplastics in the water. It was part frat house, part think tank, part fever dream.

The living room of Stonehouse was perpetually littered with Solo cups, crumpled Chipotle napkins, and half-zipped backpacks no one had opened in days. A guy in pajama pants hadn't moved from his corner of the couch since I was there the day before, Xbox controller in hand, eyes locked on the screen. Another shoveled peanut butter pretzels into his mouth while debating over which bottle of wine paired best with an apology text to his girlfriend after he got too drunk and puked at her Sororityz date party. The whole scene felt chaotic, hilarious, and weirdly intimate. Everyone had their role—the hype man, the stoner philosopher, the future finance bro, the sensitive guy pretending not to care. Together, they formed a loud, smoky, oddly comforting ecosystem, which I didn't feel fully part of yet. But I wanted to. I wanted to find my place in this strange, wild mix so I could belong.

That semester, I bought my first pair of Sperrys, leaned into the Vineyard Vines wardrobe, and, of course, got my first pair of Timberland boots. I finally jumped into the Euchre games I'd been watching for months, and with that small act, became more connected, like I'd learned the language of this strange new world. The older guys at Stonehouse started treating me less like a quiet freshman and more like one of them. The change was subtle, but it mattered to me.

Chad and I grew closer, too. What started with casual sports talk turned into late-night conversations, shared jokes, and real trust. He became the first person on campus I truly felt at home with. We shared the same secret, the feeling that we were meant for greatness. So we started dreaming together—about making something of ourselves, about building lives that mattered. By the end of freshman year, I was excited for summer in San Diego, but even more excited to get back to campus for sophomore year, when I'd move into the Sig Ep house with Chad as my roommate. What once felt like a lonely, frozen outpost now felt like my own Disneyland. I flew home feeling like I was exactly where I was supposed to be.

Yet, under the surface, a quiet question bubbled up: *What happens when this ride ends? When the music stops, and it's time to leave the amusement park, then what?*

CHAPTER 3

The Fork in the Road

That summer between freshman and sophomore year, my friends and I were back in San Diego, working internships and riding the high of completing our first year of college. I waited for an answer to the increasingly urgent question, *What am I going to do with my life?* But no clarity came. Instead, a cosmic breadcrumb showed up. His name was Oliver Steele.

Oliver's uncle was one of my dad's closest friends, and I'd met Oliver once before. Now, after a year of solo travel, he was living with my family for the summer while interning in San Diego. A few years older and seemingly wiser, Oliver had a quiet presence that suggested he'd *seen* things. He was tall and lean with shaggy blond hair, piercing blue eyes, and artistic tattoos that hinted at stories from the road.

Oliver had been on the classic Ivy League track—captain of the rowing team, everything lined up—until just before senior year, when he hit pause to travel the world. He didn't entirely reject the system; he just questioned it. I admired that. There was something magnetic about how he moved through life. I couldn't wait to hear about his travels and ask questions.

Rather than tell me about his breakthroughs, he decided to show me. One night, we shared a small dose of magic mushroom chocolate. I didn't fully understand what I was stepping into, but I was curious. I would learn the depth and medicine of that experience, which happened at the perfect time in my life. It's certainly not for everyone, but the experience was profound for me.

We wandered down to the beach beneath a full moon that hung like a lantern over the water, painting the ocean silver. The air was cool and salted, each breath thick with mist. We sat at the water's edge, knees pulled to our chests, watching waves unspool across the sand and listening to the Pacific humming its endless refrain.

I reached for my phone to play some music to add to the vibe, but Oliver gently nudged my hand down.

"Shhh," he said. "Just listen."

I paused, confused for a moment, then put the phone away. At first, all I could hear was the tide. But the longer I sat, the more I heard. The usual rhythm of water on sand began to layer. I wasn't just hearing waves anymore. The entire beach became an orchestra. The sky above pulsed with invisible geometry, constellations flickering faintly in rhythm. The cold sand beneath our feet glittered like stardust. Even the movement of the sandcrabs sent vibrations that I swear I could feel. The night wrapped around us and welcomed us in. That moment felt sacred, as if everything around me was alive and aware, moving together in one quiet, perfect symphony. And for the first time, I was part of it.

"Dude," I whispered, eyes wide. "It's like the beach is breathing."

Oliver nodded and smiled like a kindergarten teacher proud that their student had just discovered the color blue. "It *is*."

That summer, we dove into cosmic conversations about philosophy, God, meditation, music, psychedelics, and the in-between spaces that usually go unspoken. Our talks stretched late into the night and reached depths I didn't know I craved. Oliver was a catalyst, a mirror, a map. He gave me permission to explore, to be curious, to consider ideas I'd once dismissed as too "woo woo" for someone like me. Through our conversations and experiences, a quiet spirituality began to stir—a lived experience of connection to something more. I started to think outside the box, to color outside the lines, to question my assumptions, and move at a different pace.

By summer's end, Oliver returned to finish his senior year on the East Coast, and I went back to Ohio. But I wasn't the same. A copy of *Lao Tzu* came back with me. Instead of trying to fit the preppy Midwestern mold, I leaned into the new version of me. I swapped Sperrys for Vans again and brought back my backwards hat. I spent more time outside, barefoot, wandering campus with a new awareness that nature is alive and offering a standing invitation to a sacred dance.

Sophomore year started fast. Chad and I moved into the basement of the Sig Ep house on Church Street, right in the middle of town. The place reeked of stale beer and week-old trash. Febreze barely masked the smell. But beneath the chaos, Chad and I were aligned. We didn't know what we wanted to do with our lives, but we knew we didn't want to play small. We believed we were here to do something meaningful—to thrive, not just survive. We sang the lyrics of Kid Cudi's *Pursuit of Happiness* with new passion. "Tell me what you know about dreaming, dreaming, you don't really know about nothing, nothing."

That dreamer mindset started to catch on. People dropped by often, drawn to the energy. Danny was a regular. Ryland came occasionally, intrigued but still a bit guarded. There was something magnetic about dreaming out loud.

One frequent visitor was Ricky Bodner, a close friend of Chad's from back home. Though in a different fraternity, he quickly became an important part of the crew. Tan, with short brown hair and a serious, thoughtful expression, Ricky always looked like he was trying to decode life. He spoke with conviction and matter-of-factness that invited trust, and he asked the kinds of questions—about God, meaning, and self—that pushed every conversation deeper.

We spent hours imagining our futures. Chad wanted to work in sports, maybe as an agent. I dreamed of starting a company of my own one day. We had no roadmap, just a shared sense of something bigger calling. We spoke of our dreams so often that we actually began to believe they could come true.

But back then, we were pretty much all talk. We smoked weed daily with our bong named Richard Parker, and drank four to five nights a week. We rarely slept and barely exercised. There was no yoga studio within one hundred miles of campus, so my body ached once again. My diet was Will's Pizza and the $5 combo from Johnny's Liquor: a chicken parm sub, chips, and a soda delivered to the door in exchange for a crumpled five-dollar bill.

And then the campus bulletin board lit up with flyers:

THE JOB FAIR IS COMING.

All around me, students were polishing resumes and pulling wrinkled suits out of the backs of their closets. It was only my sophomore year, but you'd think graduation was next week. The Job Fair was here—and with it, a campus-wide sprint toward *the plan*.

Lock down a summer internship. Crush it. Get invited back after junior year. Land the offer. Sign early. Graduate with certainty. Climb the ladder and retire with a nice 401k and a house in Florida. That was the path. It was safe, proven, and predictable.

But I couldn't bring myself to follow it.

I didn't know exactly what I *did* want, but I knew it wasn't that. Not the conveyor belt. Not the climb up a ladder I didn't remember choosing. Not the slow trade of dreams for a paycheck and a view I wasn't even sure I wanted.

Maybe it was because nothing about my upbringing had been ordinary. My parents had raised us to ask different questions, to take different roads. And that shift really began the summer they canceled our vacation to Italy for a volunteer trip to Ethiopia and Kenya.

It's one thing to see poverty in pictures. It's another to stand in it. I'll never forget that trip we took together when I was in the eighth grade.

"Please, come in," Mama Jane said, beaming as she welcomed my family into her hut made of mud and dung. Flies landed on her cheeks, but she didn't flinch. She radiated strength wrapped in vibrant cloth, glowing in the sun. Inside, through slow and broken English, she shared how life had changed since her village gained access to clean water. Then she invited us on the water walk she used to take every day: two miles each way to a muddy river shared with animals and laundry.

Trying to impress, I volunteered to carry two four-gallon jerricans. I didn't make it halfway before I was breathless, arms shaking. A young girl in a blue sweater strolled past, giggling, and took one from my hand in stride, then she effortlessly kept walking ahead of me.

I turned to Mama Jane. "How often did you do this?"
She smiled softly. "Every day. Two times, three times."
For her, it wasn't a hardship. It was life.

That moment shook me. I couldn't unsee the contrast between her world and mine. Why did I have clean water at the tap, and so many others didn't? Why did I get to go to school, while girls my age in this village spent their days walking for water?

Guilt turned into purpose. I didn't just *want* to help—I *had* to.

When we returned home, our family sat around the kitchen table and brainstormed ways to make a real impact. We considered starting a charity, but my dad—an entrepreneur—saw flaws in the traditional model: too many half-finished projects, not enough sustainability. So we tried something different.

Inspired by companies like TOMS Shoes and Newman's Own, we launched Nika Water, a bottled water company that donated 100% of its profits to clean water projects around the globe. *Nika* means "to give" in Zulu. That became our mission.

Still in high school, I wrapped my car with the Nika logo and started delivering cases of water, pitching stores, and working farmers' markets and street fairs. I learned how to talk to people, sell a product, get rejected, and keep going. Our story inspired our community. My older sister and I gave a TEDx Talk, appeared on a segment filmed for *60 Minutes*, and spoke to students across the country about social entrepreneurship. Over five years, Nika funded clean water for more than 32,000 people.

That experience lit a fire. I didn't just want to be an entrepreneur—I wanted to *build things that mattered*.

That drive was shaped at home. Mom, an immigrant from Morocco, had built a company with her siblings that helped them live the American dream. Dad ran multiple businesses and treated entrepreneurship like a family sport.

Every Thursday night, my family watched *Shark Tank* together—not just for fun, but like a film study. Dad would hit pause after the pitch and quiz us: "If they're offering 10% for $100,000, what's the valuation?" One friend joked that it was like watching football with Tom Brady, breaking down every play.

I knew even then: *I want to pitch to the Sharks someday.*

When Nika was forced to close, my dad launched Suja Juice, a cold-pressed juice company that started in the back of a nightclub kitchen with one press. After he met a vegan chef who was making this delicious juice, Dad saw that he could help turn it into a big company. He threw himself into it—working 20-hour days, driving trucks, stacking pallets, and solving every problem himself. He liked to say business years were like dog years, because one felt like seven. I watched the endless demands age him, but I also saw how alive it made him.

One Thanksgiving, after our annual family football game, my dad asked me to help prep a shipment at the warehouse. I obliged, thinking it would be a quick few minutes. Instead, I spent hours in the cold, refrigerated warehouse, operating a forklift (against all regulations), arranging pallets by the door for pickup. On the way home, I asked, half-joking, "Do most people do this on Thanksgiving?"

Dad smiled. "No. But if you want what most people don't, you've got to be willing to do what most people won't."

Then he added, "And believe it or not, this is the fun part. The behind-the-scenes work makes the summit that much better."

I never forgot that.

Another time, I was watching Sunday Night Football when he tapped my shoulder. Suja had just landed its biggest order yet, and they were short-staffed. "Just a couple hours," he promised, though I had learned better by then.

I suited up and headed to the Suja kitchen, where I pressed bin after bin of carrots, lemons, and ginger. Every time I finished a bin, new bins kept appearing. My sister Nina worked the other side of the machine, clearing pulp and switching containers. We worked straight through the night to get the order fulfilled.

At 7:00 a.m., Mom met us at Denny's with fresh clothes so we could eat breakfast and go straight to school. I was exhausted but weirdly proud. Nina and I didn't whine about it. We *did the work*. That was just how we were raised.

Those early years—Mama Jane's walk, Nika's mission, long nights at Suja, and breakfasts at Denny's—taught me that impact doesn't come from good intentions alone. It comes from showing up, doing what others won't, and believing that the work matters.

So as I sat in my room in the fraternity house thinking about the job fair, that route just didn't seem to offer a viable path for me. I needed some advice, and in that moment I knew who to turn to—Dad.

I call him up. My voice dropped into a quiet place.

"Dad, I don't know," I said. "I just... I can't see myself going corporate. I can't fake it."

There was a pause. Then, without judgment, he replied, "Yeah, I get that. Especially after Nika and Suja, I wouldn't expect you to. That's not your road. The job fair isn't where you're going to find your path. I wouldn't worry about it. Especially if you're thinking California after college."

I felt a wave of relief hit me. Hearing someone I trusted as much as Dad say those words gave me the courage to listen to what I already knew. Dad *saw* me and saw the potential in me, and he gave me permission to trust myself. Just as Mom was there to answer the call when I needed her the most, so was Dad.

Seemingly, every other business school student turned left, but I veered right.

I didn't know where that decision would take me, but I felt there was going to be a breadcrumb for me. Earlier that semester, I'd enrolled in a social media marketing class on a whim, and it became the first college course I genuinely looked forward to. I remember sitting on the edge of my seat during a lecture on Facebook's EdgeRank algorithm, completely locked in. The class was part of a new program called Interactive Media Studies, a rogue offshoot of the business school that explored how digital tools were transforming marketing, branding, and culture. Everything about it felt fresh, experimental, and learning about that aspect of business made me feel alive.

The professor strolled in late each day wearing jeans and a worn-out T-shirt, and he carried in a can of Mountain Dew that seemed to electrify his wild hair and thick glasses. It was a whole mad-genius vibe. There were no textbooks; everything changed too fast to be written down in books. He'd drop a gem of insight, then move on like it was nothing. The class felt less like a lecture and more like a portal to the future.

One day, he mentioned that applications were open for the San Francisco Internship Program, a twelve-person cohort that spent the semester living in the city, each working their own full-time internship from Monday through Thursday. Fridays were reserved for field trips to Silicon Valley startups, tech giants, and VC firms to hear from alumni now sitting in C-suite roles at companies like Google, Instagram, Uber, and Snapchat.

As the professor described the program, that inner voice came rushing back. *YES*, it said, echoing through me, a full-body pulse of certainty that this was my next step. I applied immediately and got accepted for the fall semester.

But as the date crept closer, hesitation began to slip in.

By the end of sophomore year, I'd finally found a sense of home in Oxford. After feeling like an outsider for so long, now I didn't want to leave. I had close friends, I'd just started dating a girl, and the fraternity finally felt like mine. Leaving meant stepping away from all of it and going back into the unknown.

Still, I knew: if I wanted something different, I had to *do* something different. I couldn't keep dreaming from the comfort of the basement.

So I said *yes*.

I said goodbye to Ricky, Chad, Danny, and Ryland and traded the cornfields of Ohio for the streets of San Francisco.

I left behind everything familiar and followed the pull of curiosity.

For the first time, I truly understood the power of Robert Frost's words:

> Two roads diverged in a wood, and I—
> I took the one less traveled by,
> And that has made all the difference.

I just hoped it would make all the difference. I had no idea how much that choice—this sharp turn on the trail of following the breadcrumbs—would change my life. But I trusted the step.

And so I took it.

CHAPTER 4

Training Camp

"Are you an intern too?" I asked the woman next to me in the boardroom on the first day of employee orientation in San Francisco.

She laughed kindly and confidently, taking it as a compliment.

"No," she said, brushing a strand of dark hair behind her ear. "I just finished my master's. I'm starting full-time today."

"Oh," I said, suddenly aware of my button-down shirt that didn't quite fit and my knockoff leather notebook. "Cool, cool."

I looked down at my paper coffee cup, watching the steam curl up like it was trying to escape through the ceiling. Part of me wanted to escape, too. I took a sip, letting the caffeine spark through my brain. Around me, the other new hires quietly made small talk, all of them dressed in a way that looked professional.

The boardroom buzzed with fluorescent light. Everything was white—the coffee table, the walls, the startup-issued MacBooks. The atmosphere looked sterile and felt important. Orientation reminded me of the first day of college, that same uneasy energy of being the newbie in a place where everyone else already seemed to belong. Only this time, it wasn't Ohio. It was San Francisco.

The company was *Juicero*, a pre-launch startup building a sleek, countertop cold-press juicer, founded by health food visionary Doug Evans. Doug's energy was larger than life—charismatic, obsessive, and unapologetically mission-driven. With wiry curls, thick black-framed glasses, and a rapid-fire New York accent, he seemed more cartoon than CEO. But beneath the eccentric exterior was a sharp operator with a relentless vision. He moved with urgency, thought in absolutes, and carried the conviction of someone who truly believed he was building the next revolution in health. Every email he sent ended in all caps: *HAVE THE BEST DAY EVER*. Doug had raised $120 million from high-profile investors like Google Ventures, Kleiner Perkins, and various celebrities—people betting on him to build the next billion-dollar brand.

I felt like I had landed on another planet, a planet where I didn't speak the language—yet.

At first, the work was slow. As a marketing intern at a pre-launch company, there wasn't much to market. Most days, I sat at my desk trying not to look awkward, missing my college friends, living vicariously through snapchats from Chad and FaceTime calls with Ricky, two of the friends I stayed closest to from afar. I wondered if I'd made the wrong call.

Something had pulled me west—that same quiet inner voice that had nudged me to go back to Ohio when transferring made more sense. So I knew I was here for a reason. Then, it whispered again.

Lean in. Show up. Say yes.

So I did.

If someone needed help with a presentation, I offered it. Whether it was photos, formatting, shipping, testing, or any other task that needed attention, I jumped in. I started popping between departments, absorbing everything I learned like a sponge. I didn't care if it wasn't technically "marketing." My goal was to be useful.

By saying *yes*, I started to see how everything worked—the real, behind-the-scenes engine of a venture-backed company. I worked with industrial designers, ops teams, and UX leads. I even became Doug's unofficial green juice delivery guy.

I gravitated toward the head of operations, Sam Miner. Sam always looked like he'd just stepped off a movie set with his motorcycle jacket, slicked-back hair, and calm intensity. He held me to a higher standard, expected precision, and treated me like a peer. His quiet mentorship was another breadcrumb, reminding me I could belong in a place like this.

I didn't realize it at the time, but those early days of saying *yes* and working closely with Sam were shaping me and rewiring how I thought about work, effort, and excellence.

One night, working late, I noticed a group entering the office. A few men in suits led the way. Doug, our CEO, was accompanied by a tall man whose giant presence instantly changed the energy of the room. Since I was one of the only people still working in the office, Doug waved me over.

"Josh," he said, "meet my good friend Tony."

We shook hands. Tony's hand swallowed mine.

"Great to meet you, Josh!" he boomed.

But what really struck me wasn't his voice; it was his presence. He looked at me in a way that made me question if anyone else had ever looked at me before. I shrugged it off and got back to work at my desk.

After they had moved on to another room, someone told me who he was.

"Dude… that was Tony Robbins."

I blinked. "Tony who?"

After a quick Google search, I downloaded his book *Awaken the Giant Within* that very night, and it lit a fire in me. This is how I was introduced to Tony Robbins and the world of personal development.

The Universe is cheeky like that, sometimes. I dove headfirst into books, podcasts, and TED Talks, devouring anything I could get my hands on. I was spiritually waking up, intellectually stimulated, but physically, I was still stuck. My body felt inflamed, sluggish, and out of shape.

Fortunately, the company kitchen was unlike anything I'd seen. Each day, fresh produce from the farmers' market was transformed into colorful, nourishing, plant-based meals. It wasn't just food—it was fuel, art, and medicine. I hadn't planned to go vegan, but for three months, that's exactly what happened. And it changed everything. My skin cleared, my energy returned, and the brain fog lifted. I felt lighter, sharper, and stronger. For the first time, my body was catching up to the clarity I was feeling inside.

Around the same time, Ricky was diving into his own personal development journey, so we had each other to lean on from afar. He respected my decision to step off the traditional path and wanted to be part of it. We challenged each other to sign up for an Olympic-distance triathlon—something that would push us both beyond our comfort zones and, for me, create the structure and accountability I needed to get in shape. You can't fake your way through a triathlon. You either show up ready or you don't.

I trained hard. I watched my body transform and shed the weight I'd carried through college. I no longer crashed in the afternoons. I used to believe that fatigue was just part of life, but with real food and consistent movement, I unlocked an energy I didn't know existed. This lifestyle change translated to me finding a groove at work, too, and I became fully utilized, engaged in the work, and enjoyed contributing to the team. The fall flew by.

When Ricky showed up for the triathlon as the semester drew towards a close, I was in the best shape of my life. We swam, biked, and ran across that finish line exhausted, proud, and fully alive.

Driving back, endorphins still high, I finally said out loud what I had been thinking.

"Dude, I don't think I'm going back to school next semester. Juicero wants me to stay through the spring launch, and I have enough credits to still graduate on time. I'm just now hitting my stride out here. I need more time."

Ricky paused, then nodded. "Well, if you're not going back, then I'm not either. I'm coming to San Francisco."

A week later, he enrolled in online classes—unheard of in our pre-COVID world—and moved in, claiming the pull-out couch in my studio apartment as his new home. With Ricky there, our personal development efforts kicked into another gear.

Two Ohio kids trading college parties for yoga mats, protein shakes, and late-night talks about psychology, we created momentum together. What started with triathlon training turned into a way of life that was about more than just physical transformation. We signed up for a 200-hour yoga teacher training—and, naturally, added a bonus 50-hour certification just because we could.

We called it Training Camp.

Every day began in the dark. The alarm would go off at 4:30 a.m., when the apartment was still cold and quiet. Ricky would light a candle, brew coffee, and then we would make a protein-heavy breakfast to eat while we sat and journaled.

By 5:30, we were at the gym lifting heavy weights while the city was still asleep. I knew we were on the early grind when the stars were still out *after* we left the gym. Then I'd drop Ricky off on my way to the office with The Tim Ferris Podcast accompanying me in his absence.

Once I arrived at Juicero, the energy was high. I bounced from project to project: launch prep, brand building, internal ops. I didn't have a job title, but that didn't matter. I was there to help, to learn, to show up for whatever was needed.

At 5:30 p.m. sharp, I'd clock out and head straight to the yoga studio where I'd meet Ricky. From 6 to 9 p.m., we trained. Long hours on the mat, studying anatomy, alignment, breathwork, and philosophy. The learning was physical, emotional, and spiritual. By the end of the night, we'd be walking back to the car drenched in sweat and silence, ready to rinse, sleep, and repeat.

One night, for reasons I still can't explain, Ricky turned to me and said, "Wanna hit the gym again? Just a quick 100 pull-ups?" So we did. Because that's who we were then. All gas, no brakes.

Training camp was intoxicating. The structure, the repetition, the intensity—it showed me what I was made of and what I might be capable of. I was building something inside myself that could never be taken away, like forging steel in fire, each day's effort tempering me into someone stronger. When Ricky and I finished our training and became certified yoga instructors, I felt proud, grateful, and more connected to myself than ever before.

Soon after we finished our certification, Juicero officially launched. After months of hype, the product was finally out in the world. I expected champagne, maybe a late-night toast. Instead, at 5:00 p.m. on launch day, the office emptied like it was any other Tuesday. I stayed late, tweaking the website. By 9:00, I was the last one in the office.

That night, a hard truth settled in. You can't fake heart. You can hire talent, raise millions of dollars, and craft a sleek mission statement, but if people don't believe in what they're building, they won't stay late. They won't fight for it. They'll go home at five.

Days blurred into weeks. And just like that, the second semester of my junior year was winding down, and I was left with another decision. Stay or leave. One afternoon, Doug called me into his office.

He was walking on his treadmill, as he often did, when he looked over and said, "We've loved having you here, Josh. Why don't you stay?"

Right there from his office treadmill, Doug offered me a full-time role, complete with a six-figure salary, stock options, and the chance to keep building the company alongside him and the team he had assembled. I was twenty-one. This was the kind of offer most kids my age could only dream of.

But that quiet voice came back to me. Surprisingly, the answer was *no*. It was a nudge I couldn't ignore. I wasn't finished with college—at least not yet. I felt strongly that there was still something waiting for me back in Ohio. One last lap. A final chapter. I would have the rest of my life to work full-time, but I only had one more year to spend in college with my friends.

Doug tried to convince me otherwise, and he made a strong case, but I knew what I had to do.

I turned it down.

I scheduled dinner with Sam, the one co-worker I would miss, to say goodbye, and we promised to stay in touch. I enjoyed one last vegan meal at the office, then I packed up my apartment and headed home to San Diego.

Ricky and I flew out to Ohio and visited campus for one last weekend before classes ended that semester. We were welcomed like returning explorers—tight hugs, wide smiles, drinks in hand, everyone asking what San Francisco had been like.

It felt good to be back… until it didn't.

It hit me in quiet ways at first. The food scene in town was the same. Subway was still the healthiest option. The conversations hadn't changed either: fraternity gossip, social drama, loops I no longer felt part of.

The moment of truth came at a big end-of-year party our fraternity hosted. I observed people passed out on couches, throwing up in the bushes, and drinking themselves into oblivion. I looked around and felt like I'd stepped into a time capsule. One I'd outgrown.

Ricky leaned in. "We can't go back," he said softly.

I knew he was right.

I felt stuck—caught between worlds. I'd closed the door on San Francisco, walking away from an incredible offer. But, in a plot twist I didn't anticipate, I didn't fit in Ohio anymore. I was no longer who I'd been, and not yet who I was becoming.

I started questioning the inner voice that had told me to turn down the job. Maybe I'd misheard it. Maybe it had led me astray. *Could I still trust it?* I got quiet, asked for guidance, and prayed for the next cosmic breadcrumb to appear.

I already had plans to visit my sister Nina in Santa Monica, so I figured maybe that's where I'd find my next clue. I packed my bags, took a deep breath, and followed the whisper back west.

CHAPTER 5

Bending The Rules

Nina had recently left Stanford to start her own company, and she was already gaining traction. Her office was just a block from the ocean in Santa Monica, and the way sunlight poured through its large windows made it far more appealing than most offices and certainly more desirable than the view from the frat basement back in the Midwest. A whiteboard filled with sketches and deadlines stood in a prominent place in the office, where a small team moved with drive and purpose amidst phones ringing and ideas flying. The energy of the place lit me up. Nina had cracked the code to building something meaningful on her own terms.

Nina understood me in a way no one else could. She'd been translating my Josh-babble since before I could form complete sentences. Maybe now, she could help me figure out what came next.

Not only was the time with my sister helpful, but I quickly fell in love with Santa Monica, which fused the best parts of San Diego—sunshine, palm trees, the wellness scene—with the ambition and innovation of San Francisco. The sunlight, the smell of eucalyptus and salt, and the sense of opportunity in the atmosphere pulled me in like a magnet.

A few days after settling in, I called Ricky.

"Hey man," I said, "you gotta get over here."

Ricky and I soon found an Airbnb in Venice for the summer and started teaching yoga at a local studio, hosting sessions in the park, and inviting our friends to visit. Getting Chad out to Santa Monica didn't take much convincing. He had already been feeling major FOMO about being stuck in Ohio after we left. He had never visited California, so watching him take it all in was like watching someone step into a world of color after living in black and white. He was obsessed with the palm trees and wouldn't stop talking about them.

"They don't even look real," he'd say, grinning at the skyline like it was a movie set and taking photos of the iconic California license plates he had only seen on the screen.

We took Chad to Muscle Beach one evening when the sun was dipping low and painted the pull-up bars and palm trees in a soft, forgiving gold. The air smelled of salt, sunscreen, and the faint sweetness of funnel cake drifting from the Venice Boardwalk. Barefoot in the sand, Chad and I tossed a football back and forth, the warmth of the beach clinging to our feet as music floated from a nearby speaker. The ocean was calm, a mirror catching the fading light. The sound of laughter floated from down the beach—tourists, skateboarders, lovers, strangers—all blending into a single, sunlit song.

The scene felt surreal, like we'd stepped into a daydream we used to describe back in Ohio—the one where life in California was more of a far-off promise of freedom.

Chad caught the football and held it for a beat, looking around with quiet wonder. The light caught his face, softening it, like he was seeing life through a new lens. Then he turned to me, eyes steady.

"I'm gonna move here after we graduate," he said.

I didn't hesitate. "Good."

He raised his eyebrows, surprised I didn't laugh or talk him out of it. "There's literally nothing stopping you," I said. "You can just choose. Make the decision, and it's done."

I could see hope register in him, not just as an idea but as truth. The space between us felt charged, as if the ocean breeze had paused its flirting with the palm trees for a moment to join us in agreement.

In that moment, the dream stopped being a fantasy and started becoming a plan. For Chad, the dream became a new blueprint. He went home and started telling everyone his plan to move to California—his parents, his girlfriend, anyone who would listen. They all thought he was crazy. But he kept saying it over and over. Not because he had everything figured out, but because he had a *why*. He was going to believe it until he turned the dream into reality.

For me, that conversation on the beach crystallized something I had already begun to understand. Life really is about choices. Big or small, our choices shape everything. I loved being the one to give others permission to step off the beaten path just as Oliver Steele had done for me.

That summer unfolded like a dream laced in sun and sweat. Mornings were filled with yoga classes, afternoons with long walks or deep conversations over freshly pressed juices, and evenings were spent dreaming up wild ideas about how Ricky and I could somehow make Santa Monica home for good. We were living lightly, but with purpose. And somewhere along the way, Ricky made a bold decision.

"I'm just gonna drop out," he said one morning in a burst of clarity as we sipped coffee on the patio of Bulletproof Cafe in Venice. "I'll teach yoga, figure things out. It'll work."

His voice was steady and certain as always. I admired his decisiveness. For me, dropping out seemed like my best move too. I knew I couldn't go back to Ohio, but I still wanted a bit more structure, a bit more clarity. I needed something to anchor me.

I started thinking about Juicero again. LA was the epicenter of health and wellness, and I knew they had a big interest in growing their presence here. Asking for a job in Santa Monica felt like a long shot, but I figured it was worth reaching out. I emailed my old boss, told her I had decided not to return to school, and pitched a role for myself.

Let me open the LA market. Let me be your guy on the ground.

To my surprise, she liked the idea and ran it by the team. They asked me to write my own job description, so I did. And then they offered me the role.

It wasn't exactly the six-figure offer I had turned down in San Francisco, but it was more than enough to build a life in Santa Monica. The stability gave me confidence. I told my parents about the opportunity, and they supported me wholeheartedly. I can't overstate how much that meant. Their support wasn't just permission, it was belief. They didn't try to steer me back to safety; they let me discover my path for myself. And maybe that's the greatest thing any of us can offer someone we love—the freedom to try, the support that we'll be there, and the trust that they'll find their way.

But then Mom, always holding the candle of possibility, offered one more idea.

"Why don't you call the school? Tell them what you're doing. Maybe they'll work with you."

I laughed. "Mom, there's no way."

But by that time, I had learned not to dismiss Mom's counsel too quickly. So I scheduled a call with the head of the Interactive Media Studies department, who was the same mad professor who'd led me to San Francisco. We hopped on a phone call, and I explained everything. Where I was, what I was doing, what I hoped might be possible: to somehow use the experience as credit to help me graduate.

"I'm not going to say we'll break the rules for you," he said after a long pause. "But we're going to really, really bend them."

I nearly dropped the phone.

"This is what college should be," he went on. "You're getting real experience. You're doing the work. We can find a way."

Together, we created a custom plan. I would change my major, max out independent study credits, and enroll in a handful of classes that he would personally help me navigate. The path was unorthodox, but it worked. He provided me with clear steps and instructed me to check back before graduation to finalize everything.

I followed his instructions to the T.

That conversation changed everything. Not just because it allowed me a path to graduate, but because of the truth it revealed. The answer to an unasked question is always *no*. You never know what is possible until you ask. If I had not reached out to Juicero, that job in LA would never have existed, and if I had not listened to Mom and called the school, I wouldn't have received a college degree.

Simple questions and brave asks open doors. Sometimes wildly unexpected ones. Asking the question is imperative when you're following cosmic breadcrumbs, like lighting a signal flare to the universe that says, "I'm here. I'm doing my part." And, somehow, almost like clockwork, the next breadcrumb appears.

Ricky and I signed the lease on a two-bedroom apartment just off 7th Street and Santa Monica Boulevard, in the heart of downtown Santa Monica. The place had a little balcony, perfect for savoring post-yoga smoothies and late-night conversations under the glow of the streetlamps. We skateboarded to yoga classes, wandered down to the beach for sunsets, and slowly began to lay down roots.

During the day, I threw myself into the work I was doing with Juicero. The job had me zigzagging across Los Angeles, which allowed me to explore the city's nooks and crannies in a way most people never have the opportunity to do. Ricky and I continued to learn and grow personally, spiritually, and health-wise, constantly swapping podcast recommendations, journal prompts, or business ideas that would keep our dreams alive.

Lululemon, one of my accounts with Juicero at the time, was located on Third Street Promenade. I worked to secure a short-term activation where Juicero would have a juice press on-site in their store.

When I showed up on the first day of the activation to train their team on how to use the juice press, a few employees gathered around, all wearing their matching black tanks and name tags. I gave a quick overview, then asked for a volunteer to help me with a demo. A small blonde girl stepped forward, eyes wide and curious.

"I'm Cat," she said, smiling as she reached for the juice pack.

We struck up a conversation after the demo and quickly discovered that she lived right across the street from Ricky and me, in the neighboring apartment complex. She was also from the Midwest, a fellow transplant building her own version of a new life in California. We became friends right away, and she began to spend time with my friends. We all felt connected by shared values and that unspoken understanding that sometimes passes between people who are both in the midst of reaching for their dreams.

One afternoon, at the end of summer, when my college friends back in Ohio were gearing up for the start of their senior year, I fired off a text to our fraternity group chat. It was short but heartfelt:

> "Boys, it's been a tough decision, but I won't be coming back for senior year. I've got to follow this flow out here and see where it leads. I love you all. If any of you want to come visit me in Santa Monica, you've got a place to stay."

I meant it. But I didn't really expect anyone to take me up on it, at least not right away. So when Ryland messaged me right after, I was genuinely surprised.

Ryland and I had come a long way since our first interaction in MBI 111 that first day of college, but we were still closer to being strangers than we were to having a friendship like Chad and I had. And honestly, he wasn't someone I would have pegged as being on the same wavelength when it came to spirituality, self-discovery, or the path of intentional living.

But maybe that's exactly what was calling to him. I was about to find out.

CHAPTER 6

The Wine Opener

Fresh off the plane, Ryland steps into our apartment wide-eyed and a little out of breath, I can only assume from sprinting up the stairs with excitement. He tosses his duffel bag to the side and pulls me into a hug.

"Dude. This place…" He looks around at the open windows, the surfboards by the door, and the soft music playing in the background. "This is unreal."

Ricky grins from the kitchen. "Welcome to the dojo," he says, passing Ryland a red Solo cup half-filled with hard kombucha.

I hand him a blanket. "Come on, we're going to be late…"

Ryland had arrived on a Thursday in late summer, which meant one thing: Pier Concert Night. Every Thursday throughout the summer, the city of Santa Monica turned the pier into a full-blown outdoor music venue. A band would play standing over the water on the wooden planks, while thousands of people flooded the sand. Blankets, picnic baskets, beach chairs, speakers, wine, and joints supported the idyllic scene that seemed more like Hollywood than a real-life Thursday night. We were lucky to live just five minutes away, so naturally, Ricky and I had made it a weekly ritual.

Ryland follows us out the door, already barefoot and a little disoriented. Then he freezes. "Wait." He pats his shorts and checks his pockets. "Shit. We forgot a wine opener."

I glance at Ricky, then back to Ryland with a shrug and a grin. "No worries. Someone down there will have one. Just gives us a reason to meet somebody."

Ryland squints like he's not sure if I'm joking.

"I'm serious," I say. "We'll be fine."

He chuckles, half-amused, half-unsure of what to expect, but follows us anyway.

We weave through the crowd on the beach, stepping around blankets stretched in every direction while waves of music roll in from the pier. The air is warm, and the energy is high. Ryland's eyes dart everywhere, taking it all in. The atmosphere, the barefoot kids playing frisbee, the smell of sage and marijuana. This world is new to him, and I sense him expanding to meet it.

We find our spot, lay out the blanket, and crack open the chips. Pretty soon, Doug Beckman, the older brother of Nina's co-founder, joins us. Doug had quickly become a helpful guide and cool, tattooed older brother of sorts as Ricky and I learned to navigate the wild west of living in LA.

"Where's the wine?" Doug asks, staring at the unopened bottle of wine with his genuine smile.

"I've got it," I say, standing up and scanning the crowd for a wine opener.

A few feet away, there's a group of girls, one of them already holding a half-opened bottle of rosé. I walk over.

"Hey, sorry to bother you. Any chance you've got a wine opener we could borrow?"

The girl smiles and nods, reaching into her bag. "Of course. Want help with it?"

Before long, she and her friend are migrating over to our blanket, introducing themselves like it's the most natural thing in the world. Her name's Chelsea. She points up to Ocean Avenue.

"I work right there," she says. "Finance firm, twelfth floor. I can see the beach from my desk."

Ryland stares, stunned. "You work *there*?" He follows her finger like she just pointed out a castle. "That's insane. That's like a dream job. Ocean view? Do you realize how lucky you are?"

Chelsea laughs. "I try to."

He nods slowly, like he's seeing life through a whole new filter.

The rest of the weekend unfolds like a fast-forwarded movie. We take Ryland to park yoga, introduce him to our favorite smoothie spot, talk about books, ideas, spirituality, breathwork, and the Universe. He listens more than he talks, scribbling into a little notebook when he thinks we're not looking. But I notice. He's soaking it all in.

On Sunday, a few hours before it's time to board his flight, we meet our new friend Chelsea and her friends for a beach hang. The sun is dropping low, the sky is streaked with pinks and golds. The waves are big today, pounding with rhythm and force.

"Come in," I call, already waist-deep in the ocean. I swim just past the break. "You've gotta feel this."

Ryland stands at the edge, toes in the foam, shaking his head. "Nah, man. These waves are wild. I'm good here."

I float, smiling. "Trust me. You'll regret it if you don't."

He hesitates. A wave crashes. He flinches. But then, I see it. That flicker in his eye. The part of him that came here looking for something more.

He charges in. He dives beneath the next wave and breaks through, emerging beside me, gasping and laughing like a kid. Salt water streaming from his hair, snot down his nose, eyes lit with triumph, he emerges.

"Holy shit," he yells. "This is amazing."

We float on our backs with the Pacific saltwater cradling us, the sky burning orange above us. Soon, the pier lights flicker on to our right, and the waves quiet down just enough for us to breathe.

Ryland traces the shoreline along Ocean Avenue with his finger until he lands on a tall, white building nestled among the palms.

"There," he says. "That one. Twelfth floor. Ocean view."

I follow his gaze.

"That's what I want," he says, voice steady. "I don't know how yet. But I want that."

There's no envy in his tone. Just a sense of clarity, hunger, and wonder.

I look over at him and smile. "You'll get it."

He closes his eyes and lets the water carry him. "Yeah," he whispers, more to himself than to me. "I think I will."

We dropped Ryland off at LAX with a hug and well-wishes. After he got back to Ohio, we kept in close contact. Not just occasional texts or memes—we were constantly trading thoughts, book recommendations, and reflections from our separate worlds that somehow kept leading us down the same path. Ryland and Chad bonded over having their sights set on California and became brothers in the dream.

Soon, another visitor arrived.

This time, Danny Herrle reached out. Danny had become more than just the coolest kid in the frat house to me since we met. We stayed connected after I left the university, and he was intrigued when I jumped from college to the corporate life track. He even enrolled in the same San Francisco internship program I'd done. While he was there, we made plans for him to visit Santa Monica for a weekend.

From the minute he landed, our conversations went deep. Goals, purpose, dreams, meaning. The vibe of Santa Monica lit him up—the hustle, the openness of the people, the way strangers struck up philosophical conversations in coffee shops. We surfed, walked, talked for hours, and by the end of the trip, he looked at me and said, "I'm in. I don't know what I'm gonna do, but I want to be out here, too."

So the group grew by one more.

What began as a few texts evolved into a group chat, then an email thread where we all reflected on what we were learning, and reminded each other what we were chasing. Ricky, Chad, Ryland, Danny, and I shared a contagious love for life and growth, which soon spread to my cousin Isaac and Ricky's brother and a couple of other friends back in Ohio who were also catching the spark. The community we were creating felt like a quiet renaissance.

During the second semester of his senior year, Ryland was deep in the mess of a job search back in Ohio. While everyone else seemed to be locking in offers and planning their next steps, Ryland kept making it to the final round of interviews, then falling short, over and over again. Jobs that were perfect for him at companies that felt like a sure thing. It didn't make sense.

At this point, he was applying for jobs outside California; he was just trying to get a job *anywhere*. On paper, he was a slam dunk. Something unseen seemed to be holding him back. But every time he got a *no*, Ryland just kept saying the same thing: "Trust the process." Like a mantra.

And then, one day, a cosmic breadcrumb appeared for him.

He had connected with Chelsea from the beach on LinkedIn and saw that her company posted about an open role in their Santa Monica office. So he asked her about it. It was a long shot, she was honest with him about that. The role almost always went to internal transfers or previous interns. But she said she would personally vouch for him if he really wanted to apply.

Ryland applied for the job, fully aware of his chances. Chelsea pulled for him, which opened the first door. A chat with the recruiter led to a formal interview. Then a second. Then a third. And then the big one—the final round in-person interview in Santa Monica. The company flew him out and offered to put him up in a hotel. Ryland politely declined and opted to crash on the couch in our apartment instead.

He stayed with us all week, then the night before the big interview, we all went out for dinner. The air around the table felt more like we were getting ready for the Super Bowl than a job interview. String lights glowed above Ricky, Ryland, and me as we sat on the patio of a burger joint on Main Street, salt still drying on our skin from an ocean dip just before. The air was warm and smelled of grilled onions and sea breeze, and cars rolled by slowly, windows down, allowing music to spill out in fragments. We leaned over the table, fries scattered between us, talking through his game plan like it was the fourth quarter of a tied game.

"You ready?" I asked him.

Ryland nodded, calm and collected. "I've been ready."

And he was. Every moment of his story had built to this. The wine opener, the scribbles in his notebook, the daring swim past the break. Every conversation we'd had late at night about purpose, risk, and possibility, he would carry it all into that meeting like a secret weapon.

Ryland walked into that interview as himself, without trying to be someone he wasn't. He leaned into his hunger and told them how badly he wanted to make a life for himself in Los Angeles. He shared what this job would mean to him and how he would outwork anyone. He spoke about the possibility as if it were already a reality. And they felt his optimism.

Against the odds, Ryland got the job.

Not because of his polished résumé or any prestigious accomplishments, but because he showed up fully as himself. Because he believed. Because he stayed open, even when doors kept closing. That moment, watching our friend land his dream job and beat out candidates from Stanford and Harvard, taught us something we'd never forget: people respond to authenticity. They respond to hunger. And when you truly want something, when it lights you up from the inside, that fire becomes undeniable. It outshines credentials and checklists and whispers to the people across the table, *This one is different.*

The words we had repeated from *The Alchemist* so many times had almost become a prayer: "When you want something, all the universe conspires in helping you to achieve it."

And the wild part is that we didn't feel like luck had led to the fulfillment of Ryland's dream. Needing a wine opener months earlier had led to the natural next step for someone who was ready to move into a deeper place of trust. All those rejections, all the stalling, all the letdowns—they suddenly made sense. They weren't holding him back. They were holding space for something better. Cosmic breadcrumbs led him to the exact place where he was meant to be.

Since that time, Ryland has built an incredible career for himself at that company. He's thriving as one of the youngest regional directors in the company's history and is a strong leader in that role. He wakes up a few blocks from the ocean, tosses his board into the back of his car, and catches a few waves before work whenever possible. Some days, he walks across the sand with a coffee in hand, staring out at the Pacific as if seeing it for the first time. As if he still can't believe this life he's living is real. Then he goes to work in that office, the white one on the twelfth floor, on the cliffs with the ocean view.

Seeing Ryland trust and follow his desire inspired me. It gave oxygen to the burning embers of possibility and potential. It fanned the flames of the wavelength our friend group was on—speaking things into existence, backing it up with aligned action, and watching the Universe meet us. It was clear-cut evidence that there is a force moving through the world that seems to respond when we step toward what calls us. The more we trusted it, the more it revealed itself.

When I had outgrown my role at Juicero, the startup spark had faded, like music turned down too low for dancing. I was no longer learning, just going through the motions during the day, collecting a paycheck. That was my signal that it was time to keep pushing my edges.

The whisper came back: *There's something more.*

I had some money saved up. I wasn't worried about the next paycheck. But I was worried about wasting more time doing something that no longer felt life-giving. Quitting a good job while on a clear upward trajectory would be a gamble since I didn't know where I was headed next. One day, on the drive home from work, I rolled down the windows to let the cool wind rush in and whispered to no one in particular, *It's time.*

I called Mom.

"I think I need to quit," I told her. "I want to take some time to go find myself. Find my purpose."

She didn't flinch. She supported the decision just as she has always supported me. But she also offered me one of those mom truths that I didn't want to hear in the moment.

"Honey," she said, gently, "you don't need to find yourself. You're not lost. In life, you create yourself."

I nodded, but inside I felt resistance. Maybe she was right, but I wasn't ready to accept it yet. Not fully. I still felt like I had to go out into the world and *find* something. Find who I was. Find where I belonged. The line between searching and creating felt blurry—and I was still searching.

I wanted to have my Oliver Steele moment, to hit pause, go travel, and experience something different, something new. So, without more than that idea in mind, I put in my two-week notice, not knowing what was to come, but trusting that this was my next step.

Then the next cosmic breadcrumb appeared as a text on my phone—a message from Sam Miner, my former coworker at Juicero. He'd left the company a while back, but we honored our promise and stayed loosely in touch.

"Hey man!" his text stated, "I'm down in LA. Have some time to catch up this week over dinner?"

Over plates of yellowtail and green tea, Sam told me about his new venture, a coconut sugar company he was starting. He was looking for someone to travel to Southeast Asia, visit farming communities, learn the harvesting process firsthand, and document the journey. He needed someone curious, adventurous, and independent to complete this project, someone who could figure things out along the way. He thought I was perfect for it.

I tried to keep my cool, dipping my sushi carefully into the soy sauce, gripping my chopsticks like I did this every day. But inside, I was buzzing with excitement. This was my ticket. My next breadcrumb, clear as day.

A few days later, after Sam had spoken with his business partner, my flight was booked. Just like that, I was headed to Indonesia.

While my friends were gearing up for their final semester of classes and campus parties, I was packing a backpack for something else entirely. I didn't have all the answers. I didn't even know the right questions yet. I just knew I had to go.

I wasn't chasing a plan anymore; I was following a feeling. A pull. A quiet knowing that the Universe was, in its own mysterious way, conspiring to help me. The same unseen current that had guided us to the wine opener and Ryland to his job in LA was moving through me again.

Something was waiting for me out there—not in a career path or course syllabus, but beyond the borders of everything I'd known. I needed to shake the snow globe of my world and see what would rise to the surface when everything else settled.

Soon enough, it was my turn to board a flight leaving LAX. This time, with a one-way ticket to Bangkok and a backpack that would be my home for the next several months. Ricky dropped me off at the curb outside Tom Bradley International; our goodbye was short but heavy with meaning. He locked eyes with me and offered one final dap of faith and friendship before pulling away.

"Bring back the answers for us, brother."

And just like that, I was alone. Standing on the curb, backpack stuffed, passport in hand. Everything familiar behind me; everything unknown ahead.

I took a deep breath and stepped inside the airport.

The trip would take me to a rural farming village in Purwokerto, on the island of Java, Indonesia. I'd spend a few weeks off-grid, learning the old-world process of harvesting and drying coconut sugar. From there, I'd head to Bali to meet more producers. So I decided to extend the trip, adding some solo travel on the front and back end—more time to wander, to listen, to see what life had to say.

I didn't realize all that would come from this journey—only that when I walked back through those doors again, I wouldn't be the same person. At least, that's what I hoped.

This was my turn to leap.

CHAPTER 7

The Return

"CHURCH! WHAT THE HELL ARE YOU doing here?"
A fraternity brother bear-hugged me, his heavy pats rattling the creaky old porch of the house that had held so many memories.

"Ah man, you think I'd miss this?" I smirked.

I couldn't blame him for being surprised. It had been two years since I'd stepped foot in a classroom and four months since I'd been in the country.

Just a few weeks earlier and halfway around the world, I found myself in a small fishing village in Vietnam. I woke to a message in my inbox. The subject line read: *Time to apply to graduate.*

It was a jolt back to reality, a reminder that I was still technically enrolled in college, even amid all these wild, dust-covered adventures. I walked down the street to a local internet café, which flickered with fluorescent lights and the sound of old desktop computer fans. I slid into a cracked plastic chair. The air smelled like instant noodles and burnt coffee.

When I logged into my student portal, no surprise—my application to graduate was denied. Every senior-year course showed a zero. I'd spent the first semester working full-time and the second backpacking through Asia.

I wrote to my professor, the head of the department, with whom I'd made a handshake deal before leaving. I reminded him of our arrangement, explained the situation, and hit send. I told myself not to think about it, but the worry clung to me like the humidity. *What if he'd forgotten? What if I'd misunderstood? What if, after all this, I didn't actually graduate?*

The next morning, I returned to the same café, and my inbox was full.

Email after email from my professor—cc'd to every instructor I'd had. Each one said the same thing: *"Hey, Professor So-and-So, Joshua and I had an arrangement. Please change his grade from a zero to a 100."*

I stared at the screen, stunned. Relief washed over me in slow, dizzying waves. The next day, I came back, same chair, same bitter coffee, same portal—and there it was. Another email about graduation, only this one confirmed that my application was approved. Every zero had become an A. Somehow, after all my detours, I was even graduating with honors on the President's List and had a 4.0 GPA.

When I arrived back on campus to pick up my cap and gown, along with my honors tassel, I sure had some explaining to do.

I was happy to be back, surrounded by friends and familiar faces. The timing was perfect. I landed in our college town just in time for all the legendary senior year send-offs—Fraternity Pass Downs, the Senior Bar Crawl, and graduation week festivities. I stayed in Chad's room while I was there, and the four of us—Chad, Ryland, Danny, and me—were inseparable. We started sketching out our next chapter.

Ryland was preparing to move out to Santa Monica for his new job, and Danny had landed a full-time position at Nina's startup of all places, so his path was set. Chad didn't have a job lined up yet, but he'd committed too hard to the idea of moving to California to back out now. He'd told everyone he was going, and there was no turning back. His plan was simple: move, work retail or bartend, and figure the rest out from there.

Ricky was set to move in down the street with his brother and two close friends, and I'd be living with Ryland, Danny, and Chad. Our plan was in motion to all be in Santa Monica by the end of summer.

Before leaving campus, I wanted to meet with one more teacher who had a profound influence on me. Rabbi Yossi and I first met during my sophomore year, shortly after he and his wife moved to Oxford to start the town's first Chabad House. Short and soft-spoken, with rosy cheeks, kind eyes, and a wiry black beard, he was both wise and youthful at once. His curiosity and friendliness made every room feel lighter. I had some stories to share with him before I left, but more than that, I needed to hear what he had to say.

Back when we met, I was drifting away from religion. I grew up Jewish, but Judaism felt rigid, full of rules and rituals that didn't mean much to me. Spirituality, in my mind, was something freer, more intuitive. Yet something about his Shabbat dinners kept drawing me back. He didn't make ceremonial dinners feel like religion; he made them feel like home.

Early in our relationship, I opened up to him about my doubts. I told him how I saw religion as a closed system, something I had outgrown, and all my issues with it. I expected him to tell me off and never see him again. Instead, he smiled gently and said, "That makes sense." I was stunned at his lack of defensiveness. Then he leaned in as if to whisper a secret, "Joshua, the God you don't believe in? I don't believe in that God either."

He went on to tell me that everything I had learned about Judaism so far was the elementary school version, the

1+1=2 kind of stuff. "If you're open," he said, "I'll show you the algebra."

It was a compelling enough case for me. We began meeting weekly. He encouraged me to ask questions, even the uncomfortable ones, and reminded me that wrestling with doubt was part of the Jewish tradition itself.

"That's what the name Israel means," he said. "To wrestle with God."

We studied the Torah together in its original Hebrew and uncovered meanings that had previously eluded me. These weren't just ancient stories; they were mirrors of consciousness, morality, and growth, and we were making them relevant to today. Slowly, I began to see that spirituality and Judaism were not opposing paths for me, but two ways of walking toward the same truth.

So now, more than two years after meeting, it's a warm spring afternoon when Rabbi Yossi and I get a chance to catch up. We find a weathered park bench tucked into one of the quieter corners of campus, where the faint scent of grass and honeysuckle is drifting from the edge of the quad. A soft breeze moves through the trees, and sunlight flickers through the branches, scattering gold across the lawn. All around us, students lounge on blankets, sipping iced coffees, pretending to study. The familiar motion of campus carries on, but here, on this bench, everything slows down.

After months apart, I tell him about my travels—the monasteries and markets, the strangers who became friends, the lessons tucked between train rides and long nights on foreign rooftops. I share how I've developed a curiosity about education, about purpose and fulfillment, and how I've started to question what success really means. I tell him I have clues now—that I'm paying attention to what excites me, to what makes me feel alive—but I still haven't quite figured it all out. I'm still searching.

He listens the way he always does, with his full presence. His hands rest in his lap, his wiry beard is catching bits of the sunlight, and his eyes are kind but sharp. When I finish speaking, he nods, lets a pause hang between us, and then delivers a line that hits like a gentle punch to the soul.

"As long as you're trying to find your purpose," he says in his slow, deliberate voice, tinged with the slightest hint of a New York accent, "you'll never be living it."

He lets the words settle. I feel them land somewhere deep inside my ribcage. Then he continues.

"Purpose isn't something you *find*, it's something you *do*. You choose to live *with* purpose each and every day. That is holiness, too. Bringing purpose and Godliness into the everyday."

We sit there in silence for a while. I watch a couple toss a frisbee across the lawn. Someone pedals by on a rusted bike. The sun warms the back of my neck. His words swirl in my mind, slowly unlocking a new realization.

Maybe purpose isn't some elusive treasure I need to chase down. Maybe it's not a grand epiphany or some dramatic lightning strike of clarity. Maybe it's simpler than that—a quiet, steady decision to live with intention. To be present. To do the next right thing. Over and over again.

Mom's voice echoes back to me—the warning she gave before I left. She was right. I wasn't lost after all. I was exactly where I needed to be.

That moment shifts something fundamental. I stop hunting for an answer and start building from where I am. I decide my purpose is to live each day *with* purpose, to move through the world with presence, intention, and care, and inspire others to do the same.

That is the practice—the sacred path disguised as ordinary days. When you wash the dishes, wash the dishes. When you fold your clothes, fold your clothes. Be where you are. Bring yourself fully to the moment. That is how you meet the divine. That is how you create purpose.

On our last night on campus, we throw one final blowout party at the local bar before everyone scatters. Danny and Ryland are bartending at the busiest spot in town, now wall to wall with friends and familiar faces. They move like pros—pouring heavy, handing out shots, riding the wave of energy with effortless rhythm, and feeding Chad and me free drinks all night. The music is loud, the lights low, and the whole bar pulses. It feels cinematic, like the closing scene of a college movie with the heroes behind the bar, the electric crowd, and the future wide open.

In the middle of the chaos, I stop and take it in. I scan the room and let the moment freeze in my mind like a mental photograph. I think back to that scared freshman who knocked on a stranger's door for a ride to the hospital. To the nights I wondered if I would ever belong. To the fear of settling at the job fair. To the journey to San Francisco, then Santa Monica, then across the world. And now, somehow, I'm here, graduating with honors, a full heart, and a backpack full of stories.

A grin spreads across my face. I've done it. I took the unmarked trail, the one with no map, and it led me here. I feel grounded—strong from the habits I've built, grateful for the friendships that carried me, and inspired by the wild dream we're chasing together. This chapter of my life stretched my imagination and taught me to believe in a different kind of living. It taught me to trust the inner voice and the whispers of my intuition and gave me concrete evidence that the Universe is, in fact, conspiring to help.

Now it's time to go. We're heading for Los Angeles to once again be the small fish in a big pond. For the first time, I don't have a plan. And I don't have a steady job. But I have a place to live, three brothers by my side, and a deepening trust that I am exactly where I need to be. And maybe that's enough.

CHAPTER 8

Ask and You Shall Receive

"So what are you going to do now?"

I lost count of how many times I'd heard that question. It always came after the easier, more fun one—"Tell me about your travels!"—the one that invited stories instead of silence.

I came home with a diploma, a backpack full of dirty clothes, and the excitement of knowing Danny, Chad, and Ryland would be moving in soon, with Ricky and others down the street. But beneath the surface, the uncertainty was gnawing at me. *What comes next?*

I was coming down from the greatest high of my life, suddenly face-to-face with the gravity of what waited beyond it. My savings had dwindled, and I needed a job soon, but I couldn't bring myself to settle for the corporate ladder. Settling would have made all the mosquito bites, overnight buses, and soul-searching feel like a waste.

Maybe I'd teach English abroad. Maybe I'd go to grad school. My mind spun with options, but none of them felt right. For two years, I'd felt ahead of the curve—choosing experience over expectation, intuition over structure. Now my peers had salaries, health insurance, and LinkedIn updates, while all I had was stories. I went from feeling like I was lapping the pack to worrying that I was back at the starting line.

I was in the infamous limbo phase: that hollow space between endings and beginnings, where ideas come in waves and pressure builds with each passing day. I filled out applications to EdTech companies, nonprofits, social enterprises—anything that sounded purposeful. Each "we regret to inform you" let me down more than the last.

The voice of doubt began to speak. *What if I never figure it out? What if I settle? What if I wasted my shot?*

And yet, underneath all that noise, there was still a whisper that said, *Keep going*. Maybe this stuckness was part of the trail. Maybe it was preparing me for something I couldn't see yet.

Then the next breadcrumb arrived, tucked inside a tattered paperback.

A few weeks before the boys were set to move west, Ricky showed up at my apartment glowing. There was a lightness about him and a genuine happiness unlike anything I'd seen from him before. He was manifesting money-making opportunities, meeting amazing people, and somehow getting offered free psychedelics on a daily basis—a Ricky dream.

"What's up with you, bro? What are you on?" I asked.

He grinned and slid a dog-eared book across the table. "Just read this."

The book was *Ask and It Is Given*, by Esther Hicks. I didn't know what to make of it at first. A woman channeling a collective consciousness called Abraham sounded far-fetched. But the words rang true. The message was simple: a stream of well-being is constantly flowing to us. Our job isn't to chase or struggle—it's to tune into that stream. There's three steps. Step one: ask for what you want. Step two: it is given. Step three: allow yourself to receive it.

The allowing part is the hardest. It requires learning to feel good before the thing you want shows up. Abraham called that step *alignment*, the practice of matching yourself to the vibration of your desire so what you want can find you. The better you feel, the clearer your signal becomes. Energy first, form follows.

Esther shared a radio analogy that stuck with me. Everything I wanted already existed on its own frequency. If my dream job was broadcasting at 103.7, but I was tuned to 90.3—focused on fear, lack, or frustration—I'd never hear it. The signal wasn't missing. I was just on the wrong station.

That realization hit hard. I had been radiating doubt, worry, and impatience. I kept thinking, *I hate that I'm broke*, instead of *I can't wait to feel abundant again*. Same subject, completely different frequency. I decided to *act as if* for the next thirty days to test this theory. I would make alignment my job and live as if everything was already working out, even when I couldn't see it yet.

Each morning, before my mind could spiral into the usual noise, I sat quietly. I imagined how it would *feel* to already have what I wanted. Gratitude. Pride. Ease. I let those sensations fill my body until they felt real. The more I practiced, the clearer everything became—not the specific job title, but the essence of it.

One morning, I grabbed my journal and wrote out my desires without hesitation:

1. I want to work in the education space.
2. I want to have a positive impact on people.
3. I want remote work that allows me the freedom to travel.
4. I want to work with a mentor I can learn from.
5. I want to be paid well for meaningful work.

A tall order. But I didn't care. I believed it was possible—not because I had evidence, but because it *felt* aligned. When I told Dad, he smiled and suggested that maybe I should narrow my list down to one or two priorities. I nodded, but deep down I knew I wanted the whole thing.

Still, I couldn't meditate my way into employment. On the third morning of this practice, a single word floated up during meditation: *Network*. Of course.

I didn't need another job board; I needed people. So I started reaching out. I called old colleagues, mentors, and anyone whose path I admired. I asked questions about their career path and listened intently. At the end of each conversation, I'd say, "Is there anyone else you think I should talk to?"

That one question changed everything.

Calls turned into coffees, coffees into introductions, introductions into possibilities. I didn't have a job yet, but I had movement. The louder the world got, the quieter I became, and in that quiet, a new voice started to speak. *Keep going. You're getting closer.*

One of those calls connected me with Jake, a young guy my age who had turned his own crisis into a mission. Over coffee, he told me his story—dropping out, traveling Central America, writing a book called *Off the Beaten Path*, and giving a TEDx talk titled *How to Replace Anxiety with Purpose*.

"The definition of hell," he said, leaning back with a half-smile across from me at a quiet cafe, "is meeting the person you could have become."

I nearly spit out my coffee. "On a Tuesday morning? That's what you're dropping on me?"

We both laughed, but the line deeply resonated. It stuck like a seed in my mind and started to grow.

Every day, there are two versions of me. There is JC, the person I am today, and there is JP—Joshua's Potential—the version who shows up fully. JP doesn't hit snooze. JP listens more deeply. JP follows through and brings purpose to everything he touches. I'll never fully catch JP; that feels impossible, but each day I can try to close the gap little by little. And at the end of the day, if I showed up as fully JP as possible, then I've honored that pursuit.

By the time our coffee cups were empty, Jake was already typing on his phone. "You need to meet my buddy Zander," he said. "I'm putting you two in a group chat right now."

Another cosmic breadcrumb. I didn't question it.

The following week, I'm standing outside a small cocktail bar in Santa Monica, waiting to meet my newest connection, Zander Fryer. I spot him before he sees me. He's shorter than I expected, but his presence is strong, grounded, and magnetic. He's built like someone who trains at dawn, dressed sharp in a tailored shirt with worn-down Tom's shoes that hint at his personality. His skin is sun-warmed, his stubble neat, his dark eyes alive, as if reflecting both fire and cool water. His handshake turned into a bear hug, and he instantly felt familiar.

Zander told me about his past life in corporate, becoming one of the youngest VPs in his company's history, making six figures, flying first class, and driving his dream car. "I had everything I thought I wanted," he said. "But I didn't feel successful."

One day, a mentor asked him, *What would you do if you knew you couldn't fail?*

That question changed the trajectory of his life. He quit his job, invested everything into personal growth, and eventually founded *Sh*t You Don't Learn in College*, teaching others how to turn purpose into freedom. Within a year, his business was thriving.

He casually mentions he might be looking for someone to bring on soon. I mention that I would definitely be interested. He hasn't said what the role is or who he needs, but it doesn't matter. Before we leave, he tells me he's off to host a few events and will circle back in a couple of weeks.

I get back to my networking game, which leads me to the top floor of a building in La Jolla, California, called Trilogy Sanctuary, to meet with the founder, Joe Caldera.

A rooftop yoga studio and vegan cafe overlook the Pacific, wrapped in sunlight and ocean air. Plants hang from wooden beams, white curtains billow in the wind, and the smell of Palo Santo wood burning blends with the warm scent of gluten-free muffins.

Joe greets me with eyes the color of sunlit water and a warm smile that makes me feel recognized. Not only is Joe a successful businessman, husband, and father, but he also has intuitive gifts that enable him to read energy. He uses this gift to help many people as a spiritual advisor. The grounded energy and lighthearted, playful nature that Joe exudes feels safe right away and draws me in—a contrast to the majority of "healers" I've met.

As we wrap up our coffee, he pauses. "Hey," he says. "We just had a spot open up for an intimate little meditation retreat I host every year on Mt. Shasta. I get the feeling you're meant to be there."

I don't overanalyze it. I recognize the feeling that whispers *yes*. Another breadcrumb. So I follow.

A couple of weeks later, I drove north alone, ten hours of open road and anticipation stirring nervously under my ribs. The timing felt divine—the retreat would end on my birthday, August 8, the same day Chad, Danny, Ryland, and I were moving into our new place in Santa Monica.

For four days, under Joe's leadership, we camped off-grid. We woke with the sun, hiked through pine forests, did yoga on river rocks, and gathered around a fire at night. With no phones or noise around, all that was left was the wind moving through the trees, my breath finding its pace, and the stillness that settles when the world finally goes quiet. Somewhere between the rustle of the pines and the rhythm of my own breath, I felt like the earth and I were getting reacquainted.

I filled page after page in my journal during that retreat. The voice inside me—the one whispering through every cosmic breadcrumb—grew louder. I stopped *searching* for direction and started *listening* for it. Joe taught us about the balance between masculine and feminine energy, the dance between doing and being. Masculine energy acts, drives, and builds, while the feminine feels, receives, and creates. Both energies are needed in our lives, regardless of our gender.

That week, I realized how long I'd lived in the push zone, forcing outcomes instead of allowing them to unfold. I wondered what might happen if I approached certain parts of life in a more surrendered, receptive state. This felt like my task, my next lesson plan of the cosmic curriculum, guiding me to let go. And I felt like this was the way toward my dream job. Joe was there to remind me a dozen times throughout each day.

"Joshua, let go," he'd say. And each time he said it was my cue to take a deep breath, drop my shoulders down, and feel my body soften a little more.

On the final day, we hiked for miles through pine and volcanic rock until the sound of water drew us in. The trail opened to a sacred spring called Mother's Breast. The air felt cool and alive, carrying the scent of wet stone and cedar with it. Water, clear as glass and ancient as the mountain herself, bubbled from a dark fissure in the rock. I sat by the water's edge, closed my eyes, and began to listen.

At first, all I could hear was the river's steady rush. Then, among the buzz of insects and the low percussion of the wind sweeping through the trees, I felt layers begin to reveal themselves and the faint rhythm of my own heartbeat syncing with it all. My awareness started to sharpen and pulse to life, and I felt as if I was somehow at one with the world.

Similar to the way I felt that night on the beach with Oliver, the world revealed itself as a living organism, and the force of life met me on full display. Only this time, no substance was altering me, only the moment itself. I felt as if I had taken magic mushrooms, yet all I had consumed was a magical dose of presence with a chaser of full surrender.

I opened my eyes, and everything was harmonizing—the trees seemed to breathe, the light shimmered with a quiet intelligence, and the river carried the rhythm of the heartbeat of the mountain. I felt it in my bones; every cell joined the rhythm.

Joe turned to me, catching what I was feeling. "Spirit is the only sustainable high," he said.

And sitting there, sun on my skin, earth beneath my palms, I finally understood.

That night, we gathered around the fire. The moon hung full behind us, pouring silver through the trees. Flames crackled, sparks rising like prayers, and a quiet reverence settled over the circle. Then, from the darkness beyond the clearing, a figure stepped forward.

An old Native American man steps into the circle, the scent of tobacco swirling around him. For a moment, I can't tell if he's real or something conjured from the mountain itself. His hair falls long and white around his shoulders, his face carved and expressive, like a living work of art. A red kilted robe drapes from his frame, beads and charms clinking softly as he moves.

Joe leaps up, grinning, and embraces him. "Everybody, this is my dear friend Thunder Eater," he says.

The man's presence filled the clearing. He laughed loud and free, the kind of laugh that makes everyone else smile. He spoke of stories and ancestors and the art of remembering who we are. Then his voice softened as he shared a poem he wrote.

> "If my life was art," he said, "I want to make it a masterpiece.
> Some may love it. Some may hate it. Some may not get it.
> But I don't care. Because it's mine. And it's beautiful."

The fire crackled. The night went still. Quiet permission to let go of others' expectations of my life rippled through me like warm rain.

That final night aligned with the August supermoon on the eve of my twenty-third birthday. We had the opportunity to participate in an annual tradition with Thunder Eater and his family, a full moon healing circle. We danced in a wide circle to the beat of booming drums. We prayed for healing for our planet, its creatures, and its people. From dusk to dawn, at least one person would keep dancing to keep the rhythm alive throughout the night. When the clock struck midnight, someone in the circle began singing *Happy Birthday*. One by one, the other voices joined in. I stood in the firelight surrounded by people I had known for only four days, yet I felt forever bound to them. My eyes brimmed with tears. I felt a warmth I couldn't explain, like I was being celebrated by a family I didn't know I'd lost.

I woke up the next morning to crisp air and a clean, blue sky. I packed my gear slowly, feeling recharged, grounded, and clear. I didn't have a job. I didn't have a plan. But I had a fresh sense of peace. I rolled down the windows on the drive home, the mountain wind brushing against my face. The world shimmered with newness. When I reached the first gas station, I turned my phone back on. Messages poured in—birthday wishes, texts from friends—but one caught my eye. It was from Zander.

"Hey man, Happy Birthday! Let's meet up in LA when you get back in town. It's time I bring someone on, and I have some ideas I want to run by you for how we can work together."

I stared at the screen, cars whispering by, mountain air still fresh in my lungs, gasoline sharp in my nose, and that faint altitude high thrumming behind my eyes. This was it. The opportunity I'd been asking for—not forced, not chased, and not manufactured. It arrived like a leaf drifting downstream, finding its way without resistance.

I leaned back and exhaled as I drove south. The mountain was shrinking in the mirror, but its steadiness stayed with me. The road unspooled ahead, golden and smooth in the late-morning light.

And just like that, my dream job had arrived.

CHAPTER 9

Find The Others

Coming down from the mountain, life shifted into a new rhythm. It moved faster, and I was more focused. The wheel of my life, once jammed by resistance, now turned freely.

I returned to a new apartment with Danny, Chad, and Ryland, eagerly awaiting. That week, Zander offered me the role of Director of Operations and Sales at *Sh*t You Don't Learn in College*. The timing was uncanny. The job matched every single box I had written down only weeks before: education, mentorship, impact, remote, and paid.

The offer was modest—$1,000 a month plus commission—but I didn't care, I was in. And more importantly, I had concrete evidence that the Universe is, in fact, on my side. Through the feeling-based practices I'd learned by reading *Ask and It Is Given*, and the visualization and meditation Joe taught me, I was learning the language the Universe speaks. I wasn't fluent, not by a long shot, but I felt like I could finally hold a simple conversation.

Work life was no Juicero, where startups came with sleek offices and venture capital. Working with Zander was raw and unpretentious. Just him and me, working out of the small Venice apartment he shared with a roommate. Most days, we were crammed into his bedroom, using a narrow window ledge as a desk. Crystals lined one side of the room. His bed, always perfectly made, filled the rest of the space.

Sales was a completely new sport to me. At first, I felt awkward, like an adult learning to speak French, but *pas de problème*, I caught on quickly. Zander's program worked, and I believed in it, which made all the difference. And selling something like this ended up being a powerful way to help someone tangibly.

Phone sales, I learned, is one of the fastest paths to self-growth. You face rejection daily. You sit with discomfort—yours and theirs—and learn not to flinch. You listen for what people aren't saying. You help them see a future they don't yet believe in, which demands clarity, presence, and patience. Though challenging, I stayed with it because I knew this was a skill that would serve me forever. Zander taught me to approach each conversation with high intention and low attachment, which wasn't easy for someone who feels everything, but call by call, I built resilience. I learned to care deeply without carrying everything personally. My efforts started to work, my paychecks increased, and I found that this was something I could do well.

Zander wasn't just my boss. He was someone I could look up to. He was a few years ahead of me, which made his example both aspirational and accessible. He worked hard, paid attention to detail, and held himself to a high standard. And he expected the same from me. He didn't let me play small. He challenged me, trusted me, and made it clear that he saw something in me. When he introduced me to people, he would say, "This kid's going to make me look like a rookie one day." That belief propelled me. I would come to realize just how much those early lessons shaped the way I would lead.

In those early days, I became Zander's test subject. Before launching a new coaching module or concept, he'd try it on me first. I got the unfiltered version of everything—productivity frameworks, goal setting, mental rewiring, identity work. These were the tools he would eventually teach high-level founders for tens of thousands of dollars, and I was getting them firsthand in the laboratory.

And I brought it all home to the cramped two-bedroom apartment in downtown Santa Monica. Our living room became a kind of space where the four of us—Ryland, Chad, Danny, and I—passed around new insights and breakthroughs like gospel. Throughout that first year together, we were alive, inspired, and completely immersed in the game of growth. Surfboards and wetsuits cluttered the patio, and funky garage sale art adorned the walls. Since there was no room for a kitchen table, meals happened on the carpet, perched on couch cushions and eating off the little rolling floor desks we bought on Amazon. The bedrooms were so small that my bed and Chad's literally touched at the corner. But to us, it was perfect. And certainly an upgrade from the fraternity house.

In the living room stood our most important object—a giant classroom-sized whiteboard that took up an entire wall. It was covered in quotes, goals, mantras, and weekly themes. It wasn't decor, it was our compass. I'd led the house through a goal-setting session based on Zander's framework, adding my own twist, and this board kept us focused, reminding us why we were here and who we wanted to become.

We tracked everything: habits, challenges, even our wake-up times, which we wrote down each night before as a shared commitment, which became a quiet competition to see who would be up first. And trust me, you didn't want to be caught snoozing past your wakeup time. Every morning, before sunrise, the living room turned into our temple. Someone stretched, someone meditated, someone journaled, or trained. We each showed up in our own way, but the energy was collective and the discipline became the norm.

Danny trained for a marathon, Ryland explored photography, Chad dove into martial arts, and I signed up for a half Ironman Triathlon. We all pushed each other, supported each other, and stayed in motion. We weren't chasing perfection. We were chasing growth. We had almost nothing but we felt like we had everything.

We shared the wins, but we also faced the losses together.

When Nina's startup folded and Danny lost his job, we caught him and reminded him to trust the process. He pivoted quickly, leaning into his passion for music. He networked hard and landed an internship at Interscope Records. It didn't pay much, so he picked up shifts at a juice bar down the street. No work was beneath us. We did whatever we had to do.

That internship led to a full-time role for Danny. Chad's internship at a sports agency didn't, but through our friend Cat Davis, he got a job at Lululemon and trusted the re-route, quickly landing a role at one of the fastest-growing startups in the world, which was a perfect fit for his versatile energy. Even in the face of setbacks, we kept moving. We became well-known throughout our little neighborhood in Santa Monica. It wasn't every day our neighbors saw four shirtless guys, skateboarding as a pack to yoga classes, farmers' markets, and to the ocean to surf. I'm sure we looked like a scene out of *Rocket Power*. In fact, that Halloween, we committed fully and dressed as the characters: Otto, Reggie, Twister, and Sam.

At the end of the year, we gathered around the whiteboard, its surface layered with months of ink, smudges, and the unseen impact of everything we'd written. One by one, we read our goals out loud—career, fitness, relationships, learning, income—and realized, almost in disbelief, that we had all hit 100% of them. What started as hopeful scribbles had become a lived reality. The process worked, and we now had proof.

The next day, I came across a quote that named the very thing I hadn't realized I was feeling. I rushed home, flung open the apartment door, grabbed the black Expo marker, and wrote the new quote across the top of the whiteboard in bold, urgent strokes. I pressed so hard the ink started to fade before I finished, but I didn't lift my hand until the last word was down.

"THE GREATEST DANGER FOR MOST OF US IS NOT THAT OUR AIM IS TOO HIGH AND WE MISS IT, BUT THAT IT IS TOO LOW AND WE REACH IT."
—Michelangelo

That became our new standard. It was time to stretch. It was time to dream bigger.

One of the rituals that set the heartbeat of our home was Shabbat dinner. Every Friday night, we lit candles and poured red wine, the wax pooling slowly as the flames danced late into the night. We blessed the challah (customary bread), tore it by hand, and passed it around. Then we went around the table and shared our "Rose, Book, and Thorn." A rose for the brightest moment of the week. A book for a lesson we'd learned or were still wrestling with. A thorn for whatever had cut a little deeper than expected or a challenge we were navigating. This ritual became a sacred pause. A space to reflect, speak honestly, and be fully seen.

Anyone who joined from time to time left feeling seen and heard, like they'd slipped into a pocket of time where connection was the norm and depth wasn't awkward—it was welcome. Word spread, and Shabbat dinners quietly became legendary. Friends would text, half-teasing, "Still waiting on my Shabbat invite." We laughed, but we understood.

During that time, I found a quote from Timothy Leary that felt like it had been written directly to me.

Admit it. You aren't like them. You're not even close. You may occasionally dress yourself up as one of them, watch the same mindless television shows as they do, maybe even eat the same fast food sometimes. But it seems that the more you try to fit in, the more you feel like an outsider, watching the "normal people" as they go about their automatic existences. For every time you say club passwords like "Have a nice day" and "Weather's awful today, eh?", you yearn inside to say forbidden things like "Tell me something that makes you cry" or "What do you think déjà vu is for?"

Face it, you even want to talk to that girl in the elevator. But what if that girl in the elevator—and the balding man who walks past your cubicle at work—are thinking the same thing? Who knows what you might learn from taking a chance on conversation with a stranger? Everyone carries a piece of the puzzle. Nobody comes into your life by mere coincidence. Trust your instincts. Do the unexpected. Find the others...

That last line hit like lightning. *Find the others.* This was my call to action.

I felt a pull in my chest, strong and unmistakable. I knew I was here to help people feel what we were living: real belonging, honest connection, a deeper sense of being alive. To remind people of who they are and give them permission to dream bigger. I grabbed a pen, scribbled a Post-it note, and stuck it to my computer where I'd see it every day:

They're waiting for you.

That became my compass. A reminder to stop hiding, to get out of my own way, and show up fully for the people I'm here to serve. Because *The Others* are out there.

And they're waiting.

CHAPTER 10

We'll See

On the work front, I loved what Zander and I were building. We found a niche market and rebranded as High Impact Coaching, which was focused on helping coaches, dietitians, and health professionals scale their businesses online. With that specificity, our team started to grow, and Zander invited me to step fully into coaching as a leader.

I began coaching clients through the program. Soon, I was leading weekly mindset calls and live business Q&As. I was terrified at first. I was in my twenties, speaking on Zoom to older professionals who had paid thousands to be there. But I knew the material inside and out, and more importantly, Zander believed in me. So I borrowed that belief, showed up, and kept doing the reps. Call after call, I got steadier, clearer, and more myself.

I started to love it. The moment when something I said would land and I'd see that flicker of recognition on someone's face—that was magic. I began trusting my voice and that whisper of intuition that would guide me to say something off script.

One of the most important lessons I learned during that season was how to receive feedback—the kind that stings. I'd send my sales call recordings and get unfiltered critiques from Zander. At first, it was hard to separate my performance from my self-worth. But I stayed open. Zander once shared a Joseph Campbell quote that gave me permission: "The cave you fear to enter holds the treasure that you seek." From that moment on, I started leaning in. The more feedback I got, the more I wanted. Most people avoid it; even fewer go looking for it. But once I realized that inviting critique was the fastest path to growth, it became my edge.

At the same time, I was pushing my body harder than ever—longer bike rides, running more miles, and stricter routines. Training for a triathlon had become part of my identity; I was a triathlete, and I liked it. Ricky no longer shared this vision but I was able to get my older cousin, Rob, to be my triathlon partner. One day training for a half-Ironman race Rob and I had ahead, I felt a tug in my knee. A dull ache became persistent. I ignored it, which was easy to do since I had trained myself to override pain. My body had started whispering again, yet still I wasn't ready to listen.

One afternoon after a long ride, a podcast found me. The guest's voice came through thick with a Dutch accent: *We are responsible for our own strength, our own health, and our own happiness.*

It was Wim Hof.

I'd heard of him—"The Iceman"—famous for wild, almost mythical feats including marathons in the desert without water, swimming under frozen lakes, and climbing near Everest's death zone wearing only shorts. At first, people called him a stuntman, but then science caught up. There was indeed a method to the madness. And his methods were proven to regulate the nervous system and strengthen the body's immune response in a repeatable, teachable way that had yet to be observed. But it wasn't the science that got me. It was the simplicity of his three pillars of utilizing cold, breath, and mindset for transformation. His words felt both ancient and brand new, and I wanted in.

I signed up for his free course online, tried the breathing on YouTube, and even started ending my showers with cold water. My body rebelled, but I kept going. I knew I was only scratching the surface.

Then I discovered a weeklong retreat in Iceland offered on his website.

The retreat would be led by Joren DeBruin, who looked like a Viking from his picture online—long hair, thick beard, contrasted by kind eyes and a calm presence. He was one of Wim's original students. I didn't know why, but I trusted him. And finally, everything lined up—the timing, the savings, the freedom to go.

I hover over the registration button, then that old voice shows up.

What if it's a waste of money?
What if I don't belong?
What if I get hurt?

My palms sweat. My chest tightens. The cursor blinks like it's daring me to move. Then, something else rises—that familiar nudge I've come to recognize when the breadcrumbs are in front of me and that calm, quiet voice cheerfully says: *This way.*

I close my eyes, take a breath, and click. The confirmation page loads. *I'm going to Iceland.*

Home for the holidays, I stand up from my desk and walk into the kitchen, greeted by the smell of cinnamon and roasting vegetables drifting from the oven. Mom is at the counter, flipping through a stack of holiday cards.

"Hey," I say, trying to sound casual. "I just signed up for a retreat. In Iceland."

She looks up. "Iceland?"

"Yeah. It's a cold immersion and breathwork retreat. Part of this method I've been learning from this guy named Wim Hof, they call him The Iceman."

She blinks. "The Iceman? And cold immersion? Like… snow?" I can read her face, wondering if I'd just joined a cult.

"Freezing rivers, mostly. But yeah. Cold on purpose. It's supposed to strengthen your immune system and balance your nervous system. There's real science behind it."

She puts the cards down. "Joshua, if you go outside in the cold, you're going to get sick. Everyone knows that."

I smile. "That's actually not true. Wim's done some insane stuff—marathons in the snow barefoot, swimming under ice. But it's not about the extremes. It's about building resilience and training your body and mind."

She stares at me for a long moment, somewhere between concerned and confused. "So you're going to Iceland. To jump in frozen water. With strangers."

"And breathe," I add. "Don't forget the breathing."

She sighs, part love, part worry. "Just… don't hurt yourself."

"I won't," I say, pressing a kiss to her cheek.

Thankfully, I wasn't going alone. Sage was coming too.

Sage and I met in second grade, when I was the new kid. He walked up during recess the first day of school and said, "Hi, I'm Sage, and I'm pretty much a sports fanatic." From that moment on, we were glued together—through sports teams, homecoming costumes, high school weed busts, and late-night talks about consciousness and purpose.

After college and a battle with addiction, Sage found sobriety. Watching him reclaim his life was one of the most inspiring things I've witnessed. He didn't stop there—he began helping others do the same through mentorship and holistic work.

When I told him about the retreat, he didn't hesitate. "Let's do it."

So we booked our flights. But six weeks before the trip, everything changed.

The Universe has a way of humbling you. Just when you feel locked in, it taunts, *Hold my beer!*—and rewrites the script. Just when you're flying, it reminds you of how the ground feels.

Rob and I flew to Colorado to visit my brother Jacob, who was studying in Boulder. We were chasing a weekend of powder days and clean runs. Breckenridge was perfect—blue skies, dry snow, adrenaline dumps. On the final day, we decided to go big. One last run down a double black mogul tree line we'd conquered the day before. I was ahead, flying faster than usual with confidence in my sails. I launched off a mogul and spotted a thick tree branch hidden beneath the snow. There was no time to react.

I slammed down, face-first. Everything went quiet. Then the pain hit.

My left knee was on fire. I groaned into the snow, unable to move. I shouted to Rob and Jacob, who navigated toward me. I couldn't put weight on it. Ski patrol took nearly an hour to extract me through the trees—certainly the trickiest rescue of their day.

As they sledded me cautiously down the slope, eyes watching me from every lift and run, a thought surfaced through the haze of pain that surprised me: *I can't wait to see what good this will lead to.*

Maybe the years of mindset work had started to take root. I didn't panic, I trusted the fall meant something. An old story I'd heard drifted into my mind like snow on the wind.

A farmer's horse runs away.
The neighbors say, "What bad luck."
He replies, "We'll see."

The horse returns with two more.
"What good luck."
"We'll see."

His son breaks his leg riding one.
"How unfortunate."

"We'll see."

The army comes to draft young men,
but passes over the injured son. "Such fortune!"
The farmer smiles. "We'll see."

Back in town, I got my knee checked. It wasn't my ACL, but I had torn my MCL. No surgery was needed, but healing would take months of slow, steady recovery. Iceland was off the table. I felt completely gutted—back in a hospital bed, staring at another long road ahead. As much as I wanted to believe this detour had meaning, I could feel old patterns creeping in. The ones telling me *I'm broken* that I thought I'd outgrown. I closed my eyes, letting the steady beep of the monitors lull me into a familiar defeated fog.

But the Universe doesn't knock you down without offering a way forward. It always leaves a breadcrumb. That breadcrumb was named Sofia Costa.

I first met Sofia a year earlier at one of our earliest workshops with Zander. There were only four of us in the room. Sofia stood out immediately—short, athletic, Puerto Rican, with long brown hair in a loose ponytail. Her laugh burst straight from her chest, loud and contagious, and she moved with the calm certainty of someone who knew exactly who she was.

At dinner the night before the workshop when we first met, I cracked my back out of habit. Sitting next to me, she raised an eyebrow.

"You do that a lot?"

"All the time," I said. "My back's been a mess for years."

"Stop doing that. It's not helping. And it's not your back."

I froze. She read the look on my face.

"Come see me. I can help."

Sofia was a Doctor of Physical Therapy with a private practice in LA and a gift for reading bodies like stories. She also had suffered from compartment syndrome, the same rare injury that I had that nearly cost me my leg at age seventeen. We pulled up our pant legs and compared matching scars, which formed an instant bond.

A few days after the workshop, I walked into her office. She watched me squat, walk, and move. Then circled me slowly, studying everything.

"Left knee injury about five years ago. Left ankle when you were a kid. Right shoulder more recently."

I stared at her. "How do you know that?"

She stated plainly. "I'm watching your body talk to me."

In thirty minutes, she changed my understanding of my body. The pain wasn't the problem—it was the alarm. She connected everything: the imbalances, the injuries, the compensation patterns I hadn't been aware of, and that no other doctor or physical therapist had seen. For the first time, I felt fully seen. Other doctors gave me pills and stretches. Sofia gave me a path. But it started somewhere deeper.

"It starts with your relationship to your body," she said.

That line gave me permission to open up. I told her, quietly, that sometimes I feared I'd be in a wheelchair by thirty. That my body was broken. That I didn't know how to trust it anymore.

She looked me in the eyes and said, without blinking, "That is not your story. You're going to heal. But you have to start believing that."

She lent me her certainty when I had none of my own. We started to work together regularly, and I slowly began to trust my body again and see results. The pain didn't just fade—it transformed. It became a signal rather than a sentence.

So when I tore my MCL on the ski slope, Sofia was the first person I called.

"I think I have to cancel Iceland," I said, dejected.

There was a pause on the line.

"No," she said. "You're going to Iceland."

She didn't say it like a suggestion. She said it like a truth. Like the journey had already begun.

Sofia lived just down the street in Santa Monica. She started having me over several times a week. Her living room doubled as a studio, the table set between a couch and a bookshelf. She guided me through movement, breathwork, and energetic recalibration, bringing in her gifted intuitive healing modalities and Eastern Medicine.

Within a week, the swelling was down. A few days later, I was walking without crutches. I was healing, and healing fast. By the time the trip arrived four weeks later, I wasn't pain-free—but I was strong enough to go, leaving the doctor's ten-to-twelve week recovery estimate in the dust. When Sage and I boarded our flight to Iceland in March of 2019, I felt giddy with excitement about cold plunges and breathwork as the next hack I could introduce into my life.

But the Universe had other curriculum in mind.

CHAPTER 11

The Call of The Edge

We land in Iceland at six in the morning, stepping off the plane into air so cold and crisp that hits like a wave of clarity. It's still dark. A taxi picks Sage and me up and carries us toward the retreat center.

As the sun rises, I watch the landscape shift into something otherworldly. Volcanic rock stretches to the horizon like the surface of Mars. The earth burns deep red in places, patched with snow that glitters like crystal. We pass glacial rivers so blue they seem to glow from within.

Ninety minutes later, we arrive at an old Boy Scout lodge tucked into a valley between two steep mountains. A frozen lake gleams in the distance. The rest of the group is already in the yoga room, beginning the morning session. Before we even reach for our bags, a man steps out to greet us.

"Josh. Sage. Welcome." His voice is steady, each syllable measured and deliberate.

"I'm Joren," he says, his Dutch accent clear and clipped.

He's exactly how I pictured him: a mane of brown hair pulled into a bun, a full beard that could belong to a Norse god or mountain mystic. Thin but strong. His soft eyes contrast with his sharp features. He steps forward and gives each of us a firm, grounding hug. There's a quiet warmth in his strength that puts me instantly at ease.

Joren steps aside, smiling. "We're just getting started in the yoga room. Leave your bags outside and come in. We're about to begin a very special breathing journey." He smiles like he knows something we don't. There's a slowness to the way he speaks, a deep presence that immediately softens me, taking me back to Mount Shasta with Joe.

We drop our bags by the front door and walk toward the yoga dome, a separate wooden building off to the side of the main lodge. Inside, warmth wraps around us like a blanket, and a fire crackles in the corner. We're the last to arrive—eighteen people are already stretched across mats, eyes closed, surrendered to stillness. Joren quietly gestures to two open spaces in the back row, then takes his place at the front.

Sage and I slip in without a word. I lie down, exhaling the last traces of airport energy from my chest. My eyes close. And just like that, I'm in it.

Joren moves through the room with an energy that's hard to explain. Like an interpretive dancer, he glides and gestures as if conducting the space itself. Every movement feels deliberate. Every pause is meaningful. His voice lowers to a whisper—slow, steady, and quiet in tone, but somehow commanding. I am hanging on his every word. This is a different kind of leadership, not someone repeating what they've been taught, but true embodiment on display.

He invites us to begin the session with long, deep, rhythmic breaths.

"Fully in… and let go." "Again. Fully in… and let go."

The breath rises from my belly to my chest, cresting like a wave, then falls away. At first, I stay near the surface, simply following his voice. In and out. In and out. Then the pace quickens, like wind stirring through trees. Joren encourages us to follow the breath wherever it leads. "Whatever arises, let it. Don't think—feel."

Tingling sparks in my hands and spreads up my arms like static electricity. A sharp, citrusy buzz lights up my cheeks—like biting into a lemon. It moves behind my eyes and vibrates through my skull, reaching places I didn't know I could feel. I feel lightheaded like I could almost pass out. A flicker of doubt rises. *Is this normal? Is this safe?* Before the fear finds its full voice, Joren's voice cuts through.

"Trust yourself. Trust your body. All goooood."

His tone is calm and grounding, like he's speaking only to me. I let the fear pass and keep breathing.

The lightheadedness transforms into lightness. I feel high—floaty and euphoric. Laughter bursts out of me, unprompted. I hear others laughing, too. Some are crying. A few scream, primal and guttural, echoing against the wooden walls, but none of it feels out of place. It feels instinctual and necessary, like shaking the dirt away from a weed that's been pulled up.

As the breathing intensifies, Joren's voice drifts across the room, soft and clear.

"Whatever comes up, breathe with it. No judgment. Stay with the sensation."

His words soften the edges of the room. His tone grants me permission to stay open, to trust, to continue.

Then I feel it: a tickle just below my belly button. Barely there, like a feather grazing skin. I breathe into it, not analyzing but simply observing. The sensation anchors itself at the site of my appendectomy scar from my surgery in Ohio, a scar from a time I never wanted to revisit. I keep breathing, gently, as though in quiet conversation with the part of me that remembers.

The tingle travels slowly upward into my chest, then catches in my throat, like something lodged just beneath the surface. I cough, try to clear it, and keep going. My breath gets deeper, smoother. And then out of nowhere—explosive tears.

Raw emotion floods in like a wave breaking through. My body remembers what my mind has buried. The fear. The pain. The powerlessness of being alone in that hospital bed and just how close to the edge of death I felt in my body. I let the tears move through me.

The awareness continues downward, stopping in my right leg at the scar from compartment syndrome. More crying. Then I trace the tingle to my left knee, where I had reconstruction surgery. Sobs rise harder. Finally, it settles at the scar under my armpit, from the collapsed lung I had as a newborn.

That's when I come completely undone.

Curled into myself, shaking, I sob without sound, releasing an ancient grief that predates language itself. Somewhere in the blur, I feel a warm hand on my shoulder. Joren's voice follows, calm and unwavering.

"All gooood. Let it move. You're safe to feel it."

For once in my life, I don't try to fight it. I clutch my knees to my chest like I'm holding the child version of me.

"Body, I love you," I whisper in between sobs. "I'm sorry for what you've carried. I'm sorry for neglecting you. Thank you for keeping me alive. I'm here now. I love you."

My breath slows down just in time for Joren to guide us into savasana. I lie still, hollow and full at once. I've never touched this depth before. If that initial savasana during my first yoga class was like peeking beneath the crack of a closed door, this was a battering ram that blew its hinges clean off.

I sit up on my mat, drenched in sweat and tears, stunned. My shoulders are dropped. My jaw is loose. My stomach isn't bracing. And beneath it all, a quiet peace pulses through me that I can still feel to this day.

I can't believe this happened as a result of breathing. Part of me wonders if Joren slipped something into the water. But no—it was just the breath. Until now, I realize my relationship with my body had been one-sided. The mind issues commands:

push through, tough it out, numb the signal. But now, my body is finally speaking, and I'm ready to listen. This isn't about recovery anymore. This is healing. This is a partnership.

As we rolled up our mats and stepped out into the crisp Icelandic air, the snow crunched softly beneath our feet, and I watched my breath rise like smoke into the morning light. Everything else was the same, but I was not. The colors were sharper. The silence felt louder. My mind and body felt pain-free and at ease. I felt as if I had been reintroduced to my own aliveness.

After that session, I became obsessed with understanding what had just happened. I wanted to know the science behind the magic. How could lying on the floor and breathing lead to such a profound release?

I started studying everything I could find—Wim Hof, holotropic breathwork, rebirthing, trauma release. I learned that these methods are designed to trigger deep emotional and somatic release. Through rhythmic exhales, we expel carbon dioxide, entering a state called hypocapnia. Blood vessels constrict, blood flow shifts, and dormant neural pathways light up.

One of the most fascinating effects is the shift away from the prefrontal cortex—the part of the brain responsible for logic and analysis—and into the limbic system, which governs emotion and memory. The thinking mind quiets. The feeling body takes over.

It all made perfect sense. And yet, breathwork isn't about chasing breakthroughs. You can't force it. In Iceland, I didn't *try* to release anything. I simply showed up and followed the breath. It showed me what I was ready to feel.

Some people cry. Others laugh, tremble, scream, or feel surges of energy like electricity. I've seen people have visions, visit other planets, even experience full-body orgasms. I once read that in Hebrew, the word for "soul"—*neshama*—is also the root for the word "breath," which started to make a whole lot of sense to me.

Then I came across a clinical study that blew my mind. Wim Hof was injected with E. coli bacteria and resisted all symptoms using only breathwork. Scientists were stunned. He trained volunteers in his method, and they, too, were able to influence their immune response so they didn't experience symptoms. The findings overturned what medicine thought was possible. The autonomic nervous system—once believed to be beyond our control—was suddenly within reach.

Another study revealed that the greatest predictor of lifespan isn't cholesterol, body fat, or even genetics. It's lung capacity. But we rarely think to train our breathing muscles, despite the fact that we have twelve pounds of them. We can survive three weeks without food, three days without water, but only three minutes without breath. It is our most vital function, and yet the most overlooked.

That morning in Iceland was just the beginning of what I would come to understand.

That night, as the sun set behind pillows of pink clouds, we stood at the edge of a frozen lake, our breath clouding in the cold. Our challenge was a full-body, three-minute immersion as a group linked together. Joren guided us through slow, grounding movements, syncing breath and body. As I peeled off each layer, I felt like I was removing more than clothing—I was letting go of armor. Then Joren asked, "Who wants to lead us in?"

There was a long pause. Then, clear and quiet, a voice inside me spoke—not as a suggestion, not as a whisper, but as a knowing. *Leaders go first.*

Before my mind had time to object, my mouth answered. "I'll go." The words surprised me, since they didn't feel like mine. It was the same inner voice I observed telling me to give Ohio one more chance. The one that nudged me to book this retreat. But now, it was no longer whispering *to* me. It was speaking *through* me.

We formed a human chain and stepped into the lake, working as a single organism until we all fully submerged. The cold hit me like a wall, knocking the wind out of me. My breath turned shallow, my body screamed to get out. But I remembered what Joren taught us: don't resist, breathe. Let the cold win.

I softened. Slowed. Met the cold with presence. The panic dissolved. When time was up, we stumbled out barefoot in the snow, howling, laughing, and certainly alive.

That night, I understood something new. Beyond the recovery benefits of the cold I had known, this experience unlocked something entirely different. I hadn't just faced the cold—I faced the way I'd been meeting stress my whole life: with force, resistance, and control. But the cold doesn't yield to force. It invited me to soften. It showed me that strength lives in surrender. The cold became one of my most powerful teachers. It revealed that when stress greets me, there's a better way than white-knuckling through it, as I always had. It gave me a practice arena to shift from *brace* to *embrace*.

We spent the week peeling back layers—of breath, body, and belief—while Iceland revealed itself wild, harsh, and deeply wise. Glacial rivers ran like electric veins through volcanic rock and snow, rainbows stretched like open arms across the horizon, and at night, the Northern Lights danced in silk ribbons of green and violet, reminding us of the magic that had always been here. The cold stripped us bare, softened us into presence, and just as we acclimated to its edge, we were pulled into its opposite: fire. In a traditional sweat lodge ceremony, steam rose from volcanic stones while we sat in darkness, breathing, singing, and praying. After nearly three hours inside, stepping barefoot into the still amber light of sunset felt like a rebirth—lungs clear, heart open, earth thriving beneath us. Each day unfolded like a living myth. And as the final day neared, we felt the mountain calling. The cold had taught surrender. The breath had shown us how to feel. The climb would ask us to bring it all home.

Our final challenge was to climb Mt. Esja wearing nothing but swimwear and boots. The doctor who'd diagnosed my torn MCL just five weeks earlier would probably have referred me to a psychiatrist if he saw me now—stripped to skin and breath, hiking into −20°C winds with fifteen others. The air was brittle and sharp, and the mountain stood like an ancient guardian daring us forward.

With each step, I repeated the same mantra: *I am strong. I am healthy. I am capable.* The words steadied my breath as snow and frozen dirt crunched beneath my feet. The wind whipped in violent gusts, pressing hard against my chest, threatening to knock me off balance. There was no room for thought—only breath, only now.

"Go for timelessness," Joren called through the storm. "Don't think about how far or how long. Just breathe. One foot, then the next. Let the journey be the destination."

Step by step, breath by breath, we climbed. No one spoke. The mountain became a moving meditation. Thinking of warmth or wondering how much farther would've pulled us out of the moment—and that kind of lapse could be dangerous. Two people panicked, overwhelmed by cold and fear, and they were escorted down.

The rest of us pressed on. Each step thinned the air. Breathing felt like sipping through a straw. Not only were my fingers numb and my face frozen, but my elbow joints became stiff and numb. Still, I repeated my mantra: *I am strong. I am healthy. I am capable.* About twenty minutes from the summit, Joren turned to us, beard frozen solid. "We are crazy," he said, "but we are not stupid." And with that, we turned back.

But it was in the descent that everything changed.

Climbing down through snow and ice, a rogue wave of fear smacked me. My body, steady until then, began to signal danger. Each step downhill sent a dull pulse through my knee and stirred that old voice: *What if it gives out again? What if it's worse this time? Who will carry me down the mountain if I fall?*

The fear hijacked my mind and pulled me out of presence. I wasn't breathing. I wasn't noticing the snow, or the wind, or my feet. I was locked in a spiral of worst-case scenarios. That's when the shivering started. Not just from cold, but panic. My jaw locked. Drool dripped. My hands stopped working. I couldn't unzip my pack. My system had slipped into shutdown. I wasn't climbing anymore, I was in full survival mode. Joren saw it instantly. He ran back and slid a jacket onto my arms and stood with me to help me return to my breath.

As I did, another voice came through. Calmer. Steadier. *You're fine. Trust yourself. You can do this.*

And I did. I steadied my breath with Joren's guidance, and my body returned online. We descended slowly and finally reached the van.

That moment showed me that even in survival mode, I could come back. The rewiring was working. I was starting to really believe that I *am* strong, healthy, and capable. The mountain never lies, and the cold never spins the truth. I gained more evidence than I would ever need to convince the jury of neurons in my patterned mind of this new reality. Fear had pulled me out of the moment, but trust brought me home. And strangely, my knee felt stronger after that, and the pain was gone for the first time in a long time. I felt totally exhilarated and completely alive.

With what little energy I had left, I unzipped my pack, huddled in the back of the van, drawing more warmth from the others than the heat trying to pump through the vehicle. I pulled out my journal and scribbled what the inner voice was whispering to me: *"Stagnation can NOT exist when you are challenging yourself. Fulfillment comes from putting your FULL self into something."*

The handwriting was barely legible, but the words were unmistakably true. There's a peace that doesn't come through stillness, but through the full expression of effort. It arrives only after you've emptied the tank and poured everything out. And when it comes, it doesn't just calm you, it completes you.

Too often, we mistake the calm that follows effort for comfort. We numb ourselves with convenience, sink into routines, and convince ourselves it's peace. But underneath, something restless stirs—not a hunger for ease, but a pull toward meaning. Every mountain, every icy plunge, every triathlon has shown me the same truth: *The Edge is where life begins.* It's where strength shows up in silence, and clarity emerges through the fog. The Edge is where you meet the part of yourself that comfort will never introduce you to. It's where you decide who you are.

The real question is never whether we are capable. We are. We were born capable. The question is whether we will rise to meet the moment. Whether we'll keep moving when everything inside screams for us to stop. Whether we'll stay soft in the face of pain, breathe through the pressure, and remember who we are when it matters most. Because growth is not a pretty process. Like building muscle, it requires time under tension. But what waits on the other side is everything we chase in softer ways—purpose, fulfillment, and achievement.

As we drove back to the lodge from Mt. Esja, I gazed peacefully out of the car window at the shimmering stars and northern lights dancing faintly in the heavens. I made a quiet vow: *I don't know where the path will lead from here. I only know I will keep walking it. I will follow the call of The Edge. And I will help The Others find their way there, too.*

Not long after I got home from Iceland, Rob and I met for a long bike ride up the coast. We rode in sync, spinning through the salty air and open silence, catching up on life. I told him everything about Iceland, the breathwork, the frozen lake, and the mountain. About how the voice of fear had hijacked me, and how another voice—quieter, but stronger—had brought me back.

"You're crazy, man," he said, laughing. But something in his eyes twinkled with curiosity. The eyes, *chico*, they never lie.

Riding beside him, I realized how different I felt—expansive as the horizon to our left, free as the seagulls skimming the surf, and clear as the spring sky stretching wide above us. Iceland hadn't been a finish line; it was merely a starting point. The real work was integrating that strength into everyday life. It's one thing to feel powerful beneath the Northern Lights; it's another to stay grounded in traffic or after a sales rejection when self-doubt shows up. Still, I couldn't un-feel what I'd felt.

Somewhere between the hill climbs of our ride, Rob turned to me and said, "Let's do a full Ironman."

We'd done a few halves before, but the full felt like something else entirely—a new dimension of discipline and edge. A 2.4-mile swim, a 112-mile bike, and a marathon to finish. It sounded impossible. Which meant, of course, he was exactly right.

I looked over and grinned. "You son of a bitch, I'm in."

CHAPTER 12

If I Really Loved Myself

THE NEXT SEVERAL MONTHS UNFOLDED IN a rhythm of discipline—work, training, recovery, repeat. Mornings began with ten-mile runs, midweeks with ocean swims, weekends with double sessions. I kept up my cold immersion practice, hauling as much ice as I could carry from the liquor store down the street to my little bathtub like a ritual offering. Each plunge began the same: breath led the way. Not far behind came the others—Presence, first through the door, grounding me; Surrender, soft and unhurried, finding her seat; and Peace, arriving last fashionably late, yet always the one who stayed the longest.

After one especially long run left Rob's ankle flaring up, I made it my mission to get him hooked on the cold practice.

"Just try it. Trust me," I told him, handing him a towel like a dealer, with complete confidence that his ailment would reveal what I had already discovered.

He gave me a look, then stepped in like a soldier. He sat in the freezing bathtub, bracing hard, slowing his breath down with my guidance, and melting into the experience. When he stepped out and tested his ankle, his eyes lit up.

"Wait... It's gone!" he said, shifting his weight side to side. "I feel no pain. And I feel great! What the hell just happened?"

I laughed. "Welcome to the club."

He shook his head, still in disbelief. "Alright. I get it now."

From that moment on, he was all in.

The ice-bag-bathtub combo wasn't a sustainable solution, given how often I wanted to plunge. After some late-night research, I discovered a Facebook group dedicated to helping people convert deep chest freezers into full-on ice baths, which would mean no more weird looks from the liquor shop owner.

Rob was the obvious first call. He was the handyman of our crew, the guy we called for anything remotely technical—jobs we'd come to call "Rob jobs." I asked if he'd help me build an ice bath in my apartment. Convincing Chad, Danny, and Ryland would be a problem for later. He stared at me like I'd grown a second head.

"So you want to sit in a chest freezer filled with water. Aren't you worried about it breaking or electrocuting you?"

"Yes, I am, and that's why I'm asking you," I said tongue-in-cheek.

"Why don't you just buy a cold tub that's made for it?"

I explained why the existing cold plunge options didn't work: oversized, overpriced, permanent fixtures that looked more at home in a luxury spa than on a tiny Santa Monica apartment balcony. Fifteen thousand dollars for a huge, heavy metal box of cold water wasn't going to cut it.

Rob paused. His eyes narrowed the way they do when his engineer brain starts clicking.

"There's gotta be a better way," he said slowly. "A hot tub doesn't even cost that much. After the Ironman, let's build you something better. And something that won't electrocute you."

"Sounds like a plan."

That was the moment the idea took root. We decided to call it Project Polar.

We were deep in prep mode during the final week before the Ironman. Our bikes were shipped to Florida, flights booked, bags half-packed. Taper week had begun, which meant decreasing my training load to get my body rested and primed to peak on Sunday. The plan was dialed.

On Monday, six days out, I step out the door for my last official run of the nine-month training cycle. Four easy miles. Nothing heroic, just a shakeout to stay loose. I jog through the quiet Santa Monica streets, the afternoon light soft and gold, the scent of cool autumn air steadies my breath.

Mike Posner's new album plays in my headphones, each lyric tracing his walk across America. His story inspired me— stepping away from the spotlight to find purpose one mile at a time. As I listen to his music, I can't help but think that someday I'd love to meet him and tell him what his journey has meant to me.

Then, mid-stride, a faint pinch ripples through my calf and shin. It's subtle, so I brush it off and finish my run. By morning, the ache has sharpened. Each step, I feel the tug. Still, I take a deep breath and tell myself it's simply tightness, nothing to worry about. I clicked into the pedals of the stationary bike at the gym for an easy spin to loosen up. The pain flares again, sharp and insistent with every revolution. There's no ignoring it now; something isn't right.

Panic begins to stir in me beneath the surface.

I call Mom. She suggested I drive to San Diego and see our orthopedic doctor. I don't question Mom's direction at this point. I arrive in San Diego on Wednesday afternoon for my appointment, and my flight is leaving the next morning. The race is five days away.

The waiting room hits like déjà vu. That sterile air. The faint bite of disinfectant. I've spent too much time in this office—braces, casts, setbacks, slow recoveries. Behind the counter, I spot Chuck, the cast guy I've known since childhood, moving through the hallway. I look away, pretending not to know him. It's not just my leg that aches, but old identities stir, uninvited. Patterns I shed on Mt. Shasta and beliefs I rewrote on Mt. Esja begin to reassemble, creeping toward the driver's seat, ready to grab the wheel

The doctor studies the scans and looks up.

"You've got shin splints that have progressed into microstress fractures."

"You're kidding." I take a breath. "Can I still race on Sunday?" I ask.

He hesitates. "If you can tolerate the pain, it's your call. But you're at risk. Those microfractures could turn into more serious fractures, which would mean a long recovery."

I nod, but inside, my heart jumps off a cliff and bellyflops deep into my stomach. When I step outside, the afternoon light has dulled to gray. The drive back home is silent at first. Then the tears come slow, heavy, and unstoppable.

How can this be happening? It feels like a bad dream from which I can't wake up.

I don't know what to do. Part of me still wants to try. Maybe I can grit through it. Maybe once I'm moving, the pain will fade. Maybe this is my moment to prove something—to myself, to everyone who ever doubted me, to the version of me that once believed he was broken. I *know* I'm strong, healthy, and capable.

But then another voice rises: *What if you go too far? What if this turns into something worse and leaves you badly injured? Do you really want to be on crutches at your sister's wedding, standing on the edge of the dance floor, smiling through pain?*

The whisper of fear blurs with the whisper of intuition. And for the first time, I can't tell them apart.

I call Sofia. Tears slip down as I wait for her to answer. She picks up on the second ring.

I pour it all out, hoping she'll give me clarity, or even make the decision for me. But she just listens. Then, gently, she asks the one question I've been waiting for without even realizing it:

"What does your body want? If you really loved yourself, what would you do?"

Silence on the line.

After we hang up, I return to my apartment and lie down on my bed. I close my eyes and start to breathe. I drop into my body. I ask myself quietly: *If I really loved myself, what would I do?*

I wait. Nothing yet. And then, like a message rising up from my bones, the answer comes.

You don't need to prove anything.

Those six words land with quiet force, like a key turning in a long-locked door. The pressure in my chest releases. My jaw softens. My breath deepens for the first time all day. I sit up slowly, as if surfacing from underwater. The noise in my head fades. I feel lighter, calmer, and clearer.

I text Rob. Then Mom. Then Sofia. I tell them I'm not going to do the race. Each one replies with the same energy of love, support, and total respect.

That question—*If I really loved myself, what would I do?*—has become one I return to time and time again. It slices through the noise with startling precision, bringing clarity in moments of doubt.

When the alarm goes off early some days and I'm caught between getting up to work out or letting myself rest, I ask it. Sometimes the answer is to stay in bed, to honor the body's need for recovery. Other times it's to rise and move, because I know how good I'll feel once I do. The question invites discernment. It reconciles the present self and the future self in a single breath. Because sometimes, love means pushing through and enduring. And sometimes, love means pulling back and letting go.

I still boarded that flight to Florida to support Rob. I stood on the sidelines and cheered with everything I had when he crossed that finish line without me. It was gutting, but I was proud of him. Proud of us. He turned to me afterward, still buzzing with adrenaline, and said, "I'll do another one with you whenever you're ready, brother."

I smiled and nodded, but I couldn't imagine racing again anytime soon.

Still, as I stood by the red carpet, watching others cross that final arch, I made myself a promise: *I will be back. And when I get here, it will be that much sweeter.*

On the flight home, I posted the most honest thing I'd ever written on Instagram:

> "I've cried more in these past 3 days than I have probably all year (and I cry A LOT lol). This week has been an emotional whirlwind for me. For whoever might need this message, I felt compelled to share… Developing shin splints in my final week before this Ironman race wasn't part of the plan. But as my wise mamma has always said, 'Man plans & God laughs.'
>
> Through this process, I've come to appreciate, love, and respect my body on a whole new level. I chose to honor my body and its healing process by listening to my intuition and did NOT enter the race on Sunday. Dancing at my sister's wedding next month is far more important than risking further injury to limp across the finish line for a fleeting ego stroke.
>
> But through facing this—and sitting in the discomfort—I've realized I didn't need a medal to make this journey worth it. The impossible became possible two weeks ago when Rob and I crushed our longest training day and looked at each other and said, 'We got this.'
>
> What once felt laughable—a 2.4-mile swim, 112-mile bike, and 26.2-mile run—had become doable. We raised over $11,000 for muscular dystrophy research

and will help make life-changing renovations to my cousin Kathryn's home. This journey has already been a massive victory.

There will always be more races. More chances to compete with full integrity. And in this decision, I feel a deep sense of clarity, relief, and gratitude. This pressure is truly a privilege—and this entire situation is the most first-world of first-world problems.

Facing this forced me to confront my deepest fear—not starting the race at all. And in letting go, I've discovered a different kind of strength. One I didn't know I was looking for.

Turns out, I just won the race I didn't even realize I was in."

It felt like a kind of graduation, as if the Universe handed me my elementary school diploma with a wink. I wasn't looking for a breadcrumb of confirmation, but I received a whole pie. Literally the following week after coming home, I went to the gym to nurse my shin, easing back in with a light swim. After my laps, I walked into the locker room and saw a guy on crutches struggling with his locker.

I offered to help. He smiled.

We got to talking. "Shin splints," he said. "I pushed through the pain and ran a marathon. Ended up with a full fracture. Three months on crutches, and at least six more months of recovery to go."

I just stood there, stunned. These are the winks from the Universe you can't make up.

Moments like that don't happen when you're charging forward blindly. They occur when you slow down, when you choose to listen. When you let love—not fear—make the call.

That was the real race. And I had already won.

Part II

The Builder:
An Outer Experiment

CHAPTER 13

The COVID Cousin Project

As fall gave way to winter and our sacred year-end reflections approached, I felt a pull to expand the tradition. Instead of guiding just Ryland, Danny, and Chad through our usual process of closing one year and visioning the next, I wanted to open it up and invite others into the practice that had become so foundational for us.

So I rented a small venue and hosted my first workshop, a goal-setting experience for 2020. It sold out. Thirty-five people showed up, ready to reflect, journal, and set meaningful intentions. I stood at the front of the room, guiding them through prompts and frameworks, and felt totally and completely in my element. Like a fish in water, swimming freely. That day became a milestone that fueled my desire to step onto the stage and share my lessons and stories to help people.

Six weeks later, everything changed when COVID hit.

That spring, our lease was ending, and it felt like the right moment to move on for several reasons. I felt the pull back to San Diego, where Zander and Rob were living. Ryland was also getting ready to move in with his girlfriend.

Our final Shabbat dinner together was emotional—each of us offering words from the heart, each of us crying tears of gratitude. Over the past three years, we had built something rare: a chosen family. Just a few kids from Ohio who moved west to figure life out, and now, somehow, we were all on our path.

Back in San Diego, life slowed down while work sped up. High Impact Coaching saw a surge in demand as coaches, therapists, and trainers rushed to take their work online. We became the bridge. Our revenue soared into the millions, and I stepped fully into my role as Director of Operations, managing our fast-scaling phase of hiring, building systems, and serving hundreds of clients across the world. We were named the second-fastest-growing private coaching company in the country by the Inc. 5000 that year. We went from leading small seminars with four people in a room to packing hotel banquet halls with over a hundred.

During that season, another dream surfaced: launching a podcast. A space to share stories, lessons, and honest conversation. I called it *Find the Others*, a nod to the Timothy Leary quote that spoke to me so much. I committed to two episodes a week, one solo and one guest interview. The solo episodes sharpened my thinking. The interviews deepened my listening. The podcast became a gym for my voice and a lab for my ideas.

My first guest was Sage. We talked about breathwork, healing, and our time in Iceland. After we stopped recording, we kept dreaming. We wanted to lead a retreat of our own together. Especially with COVID, people needed these tools and this medicine. But given the state of the world, finding a venue to rent seemed impossible. We needed a cosmic breadcrumb.

Not long after that conversation, I went to Rosarito, Mexico, for a high school friend's wedding. The celebration was held at her family's villa, perched above the beach and wrapped in panoramic views of the ocean and swaying palms.

The name alone felt like a sign: *Villa Del Paraiso*—Paradise House. The energy of the place was bright and alive.

During the reception, I asked the father of the bride, Tim, if he'd ever hosted retreats there. His face lit up. He told me about his own healing journey, how years ago he'd used the space for that very purpose. "If you want to bring something here," he said, "you can have it." His offer wasn't a business transaction; it was a gift. Just like that, we had a venue.

At that first retreat, I watched people unravel in the best way. Grown men cried for the first time in years. Others dropped stories they'd been carrying for decades. And I felt at home. Holding space, designing the arc of the weekend, guiding people to their own edge through our tools of breath, ice, presence, and community. And they were ready. They showed up with openness and left transformed. That weekend made clear that this was more than a side project. This was a calling. I decided to get certified in the Wim Hof Method, which would equip me to lead dozens more retreats, even some alongside Joren, back full circle in Iceland.

Meanwhile, Rob and I kicked Project Polar into the next gear. He successfully created a makeshift cold tub. That first model was a beat-up Rubbermaid tub with holes drilled in the sides, thick aquarium hoses coiled like jungle vines, and a clunky aquaponics chiller roaring to keep the water cold. We added a water pump and a filtration system, which only made it more absurd-looking, with tubes shooting out in all directions. It took up half of Rob's garage, but it worked. We affectionately called it Frankenstein. The cost of creating it was roughly the same as a DIY chest freezer setup, but it traded the risk of electrical shock for filtration to keep the water clean. We felt like breakthrough inventors.

I showed Rob the Facebook groups and Reddit threads full of tens of thousands of people hacking their own ice bath setups, fueling a full-blown movement. The demand was apparent. People weren't looking for luxury; they wanted something cold, affordable, and safe. We posted an inquiry just for fun, curious if anyone would actually buy our prototype. To our surprise, messages rolled in. People wanted one.

I turned to Rob and said the words that would define our partnership: "If you build it, I will sell it."

I was serious, and Rob could tell, which made him serious. So the project got real. Rob drew on his years of supply chain and logistics experience, knowing how to find suppliers, source materials, and think systematically. We found a manufacturer overseas and ordered a sample of a commercial-grade chiller that would replace the clunky aquaponics unit we'd been using.

After waiting four weeks for the thing to arrive, we were giddy like kids on Christmas morning when it was finally delivered. But to our disappointment, the chiller was cracked. Broken in transit. A false start. Fortunately, the supplier replaced it with a second unit that worked, which was our first real win.

Now we had to innovate to simplify it. I kept saying, "It has to be Joshua-proof. One box. Two hoses. No tools, no headaches. Just plug and plunge."

Our Rubbermaid tub was too bulky, too ugly, and definitely not portable. We both wanted something we could travel with, toss on a balcony, and set up in five minutes. While standing in Rob's garage, my eyes landed on a sleek collapsible cooler; maybe that foldable foam design could work. Then I scanned past a dusty duffel bag.

"What's in here?" I asked.

Rob unzipped it. "It's one of those inflatable paddleboards that's super durable, you can drive over it with your car."

We almost kept moving, but we paused. That material—drop-stitch, military-grade, rigid when inflated, light enough to carry—was exactly what we'd been missing.

"Think this paddleboard factory could make us a tub?"

"I don't see why not," Rob said.

It wasn't cheap. We needed two manufacturers—one for the chiller, one for the tub—and working with factories overseas meant wiring money upfront with no safety net. We needed to send $10,000 to get the next stage custom prototype we wanted. We weren't product developers or startup founders; we were just two cousins chasing our curiosity, trying to see if this thing had legs. We were learning a ton, and we were having fun. So despite some healthy skepticism, we sent the wire. Not because we knew what would come of it, but because it was worth it to us to find out.

The next few months were a trial-and-error period. Four versions of the chiller came and went before we found the right specs—filter, pump, even heater, all integrated into one unit. The tub was more difficult to perfect. Manufacturer after manufacturer missed the mark. But each round taught us something. We'd unbox a new sample with giddiness, poke holes in it, brainstorm how to improve it, and start again.

Slowly, our idea began to take shape. Project Polar was no longer just a garage experiment—it was starting to feel like a real product—a solution people might actually want.

This wasn't the first time Rob and I had dreamed up a venture together. When I was ten years old, we came up with "Laser Lynx"—a futuristic laser tag arena we invented during a family ski trip in Colorado. In between runs on the mountain and hot chocolate in the lodge, we sketched elaborate blueprints: custom weapons, secret tunnels, sci-fi sound effects. We stashed the drawings in the hotel room safe like state secrets. Laser Lynx never made it past the lodge, but even back then, building something with my big cousin Rob felt like fun.

Now, nearly two decades later, we were back at it, only this time, with prototypes, suppliers, and actual interest from people ready to buy. This time, we were serious. This was my chance to put everything I'd learned about following the cosmic breadcrumbs and partnering with the Universe to the test. It felt like the next evolution, a new experiment in co-creation.

We each put in money from our savings, tallying up to over $30,000. Money we'd set aside over the years from jobs, side hustles, and sheer discipline. The cold immersion wave was rising fast. The Wim Hof Method was hitting the mainstream. Timing mattered, and I could feel it in my bones—this was the window.

Before we could greenlight the first production run of 50 units, we needed an additional $50,000. We explored loan options, even got terms from a bank, but then we had a better idea. What if we pitched it to Dad?

We built a pitch deck and made our case, hoping to convince him to invest. He took it seriously. He listened, asked hard questions, pressed on the gaps. But he also saw how invested we were, not just financially but emotionally, to make this work. He agreed to the loan and even gave us better terms than the bank. We shook hands, and I felt that surge of gratitude and a quiet pressure of someone taking a chance on you.

With the final piece in place, Project Polar became real. This wasn't just a garage project anymore. We were building a brand. And now, we needed help.

Luckily, I knew exactly who to call.

CHAPTER 14

Going All In

I sat at a café just before the year turned over and 2022 began. Late December light slanted through the windows, soft and pale, while Christmas music still trickled through the speakers. Cat Davis slid into the seat across from me with that same grounded, radiant energy she's always had.

Years had passed since our early days—me slinging Juicero machines, her working retail at Lululemon—but we'd stayed in touch, orbiting each other through different seasons of life. Since then, she'd grown into a creative force, leading brand and marketing for a major e-commerce company before setting off on her own. She had more than skill, she had instincts that I knew I could trust.

As we caught up, I pulled out my phone and showed her sketches, mockups, and early prototypes of the tub. The moment I began to speak, her eyes lit up. I could see her mind catching fire, gears turning. She got it immediately—the product, the story, the potential in what we had.

I walked her through our plan for a presale campaign launching March 31, with units shipping by early summer. She nodded, already thinking ahead, and I asked her to send a proposal outlining how she could support us with branding, go-to-market, social media, and e-commerce setup. Rob and I brought her on right away, and from day one, Cat gave the project the focus, heart, and intensity of a co-founder.

The first thing we tackled together was the name. Project Polar had worked for our garage-phase prototype, but this wasn't that anymore. The whisper spoke up as if it had been waiting for a chance to speak: *Edge Theory*. The moment I said it, we all knew. It represented everything that I learned in Iceland and captured that spirit. This wasn't just a product; it was a practice where people came to meet their edge. To find what lives just beyond comfort. We named the flagship model *The Edge Tub*.

Rob suggested adding "Labs" to give it dimension, a nod to innovation. *Edge Theory Labs*. It sounded sharp, forward-facing. The domain was available, so we locked it in.

That winter, Rob was buried in supplier calls, working to refine the product and finalize logistics for our first delivery. Meanwhile, Cat and I built the brand by defining our tone, story, voice, and feel. We started dreaming about an epic launch video. That evening, I sat down at my laptop and started writing. The launch script poured out effortlessly.

> Nothing great was ever achieved from being comfortable. To reach new heights, we must be prepared to cross new boundaries. We've got to leave the warmth and coziness of our comfort zone. And nothing seems more uncomfortable than jumping into freezing cold water.
>
> No one likes the cold. It's uncomfortable. Painful. It's...cold. The cold is a mirror of our inner world. It represents our deepest fears, shines a spotlight on our limiting beliefs, and gives our mental chatter a microphone on center stage. But what if, on the other side of the thing we fear the most, is the breakthrough we've been waiting for?

Yeah, no one enjoys the cold, but that's kinda the point. It can be our greatest ally if we allow it to be...A trainer who helps us recover quicker, sleep better, think clearly, and feel more alive. A coach who teaches us to be present in the intensity of the moment, calm under the pressure, focused under duress. And all it takes is three minutes. Three minutes every day to unlock the full benefits for a faster recovery, healthier body, and stronger mind.

That's why we built The Edge Tub. A cold tub that you can use every day—wherever, whenever. A cold tub that doesn't need a trunk full of ice to cool it down every time, or constant draining and refilling to keep it clean. A cold tub that can become a hot tub with the push of a button. At Edge Theory Labs, we believe that greatness happens at the edge of your comfort zone. And we're on a mission to give you the tools that give you the edge. The edge on recovery, on your performance, on winning the day.

Whatever edge you are pushing towards, whatever goals you are striving for, whatever greatness you aspire to achieve, keep going. Because what if everything we want is just *one* step outside of our comfort zone? Take the step. You got this, and we got you...Go All In!

Chills. I felt like we were onto something, naming a feeling and articulating a sentiment that meant so much.

With the Edge Theory Labs launch approaching, the time had come to start sharing the idea and gathering feedback from people we trusted. I went back to what had always worked best: leaning on my network.

Doug Evans, the former founder of Juicero, came to mind immediately. Doug had always been a bold thinker—maybe too bold for Silicon Valley at times—and I respected his vision.

We'd stayed in touch loosely over the years. Now he was living in Joshua Tree with his wife, running a boutique hot springs resort, and dreaming up his next chapter. When I reached out, he invited us out for a visit.

Rob and I packed our one and only prototype into Rob's car and hit the road, calling it a "founder retreat." The desert greeted us with vast skies and stillness. We set up the tub beside a steaming stone hot springs tub, and soon we were plunging back and forth, grinning like kids pulling off a backyard science experiment. Our product really worked.

Soon Doug came outside and tried it himself. After drying himself off, he leaned back in his chair with a knowing nod. With analytical curiosity, he said, "You've got something here. Something big." Next, in typical Doug fashion, he encouraged us to raise millions and scale fast. His energy lit a fire under us, but also stirred bigger questions. How far did we really want to take this?

That night, under a sky so full of stars it barely looked real, Rob and I soaked in the hot springs again. The heat softened our muscles and quieted the noise. We spoke openly about our goals, values, and vision. We were fifty-fifty partners, and Rob suggested we split the responsibilities down the middle: he'd run product, operations, and finance; I'd lead sales, marketing, and community. We felt totally aligned on scaling this business.

We started dreaming out loud about culture, and about creating a company rooted in transformation. Not just for our customers, but for us and, hopefully, one day, our future employees. We wanted to create a company that *we* would like to work for as employees, with a culture of uncharacteristic doers living life to the fullest. We wanted to create a company of The Others. We pictured retreats, Ironman competitions, and company challenges. An office filled with light and purpose. I looked over at Rob, half-joking, half-certain, and said, "We're gonna be commuting into that office this fall."

He smiled, knowing it was a long shot, but said nothing the way a parent holds back the truth to keep a child's wonder alive a little longer.

It felt like dreaming with Chad in the basement of the fraternity house, only this time the dreams we spoke of were business. I felt that same knowing and belief that these dreams would in fact come true, without a shred of evidence yet.

The next morning, as we were loading the tub into the car, Doug called out casually across the driveway.

"Oh, by the way," he said. "I want to introduce you to a good friend of mine, Mike Posner. He loves cold plunges and might be into this. I'll connect you."

I nodded like it was no big deal. "Appreciate it."

But inside, I lit up—another cosmic breadcrumb, another dream coming closer to reality.

When our first branded sample arrived from the manufacturer, it still had a long way to go, but it was a special experience. Seeing the black Edge Theory Labs logo stretched across the side of the gray tub made it real, like the idea had grown legs and could now stand on its own. And the timing couldn't have been better, because we were racing the clock to film our launch video and stay on track for our projected release date.

I was back in that familiar training-camp mode, with full days working with Zander, then long nights with Rob and Cat, pouring energy into the build. I even looped in Nikita, a friend and former teammate from High Impact Coaching. He jumped in without hesitation, just happy to be part of the ride.

From the first roll of the camera, the shoot for our launch video had a magic to it. Under Cat's creative direction and with a talented videographer friend behind the lens, we created something far bigger than our budget should've allowed. Rob, Cat, and I played the roles of models, laughing between takes, yet stunned by how seamlessly it was all coming together.

The final shot we dreamed of was a drone shot of me running along a mountain ridge at the golden hour of sunset, pulling back to establish a visual metaphor for everything we wanted the brand to say. But with only an hour left before sunset, we were still searching for the right location. Every trailhead was a dead end, and light was fading fast.

Frustrated but not willing to quit, I looked at Rob and Cat and said what would become a mantra for us: "We didn't come this far to only come this far."

We tried one last place. One final trail. And just like that, there it was. The perfect ridgeline, even better than we imagined. We sprinted up the hill, launched the drone, and caught the final shot just as the sun dipped below the horizon. It was cinematic, serendipitous, and felt even a bit like destiny. We didn't just capture the scene, we captured the soul of the brand. It felt like the Universe was conspiring to make this happen, supporting us and helping us with both big and small details the whole way.

The week before launch was a blur. That week, I was running High Impact Coaching's biggest live event to date, which included eighty clients flying in from around the world for a two-day conference. I emceed, managed clients, juggled logistics, and kept the whole thing moving. But my mind kept drifting back to Edge. I was split between two commitments, pulled in both directions in the best way.

On the final morning of the event, we'd planned a wellness session in the hotel's garden. I asked Zander if I could set up the prototype cold tub. "Of course," he said.

That morning, in the Guild Hotel courtyard in Downtown San Diego, I filled the tub, connected the chiller, and watched the water ripple to life. Even though it wasn't our final product, it existed in real life. People were drawn to it. One client, Tucker, wandered over with a towel and curiosity. I guided him through his plunge, watching his body spark back to life as he climbed out.

"Man," he said, still buzzing. "I was about to drop ten grand on a cold tub. Now I know it's definitely worth it, I've gotta have that every day!"

I blinked. "Well, we're launching a pre-order next week for this tub. It's going to be under five grand."

His eyes widened. "You're kidding."

"Nope!"

He laughed. "I'm in."

That was our first real validation.

That night, after the event wrapped, Rob, Cat, and I met in the coworking space at my building. It had become our makeshift war room—whiteboards full of notes, power cords snaking across the floor, half-eaten snacks, and caffeine on every surface. We were down to the wire.

Rob was polishing tech specs and FAQs for the website. I was dialing in the final landing page copy. Cat tweaked product shots and tested Shopify with the precision of a surgeon. The next day was launch day, and we had a booth alongside other vendors for the Ironman Oceanside race, a perfectly fitting and symbolic gesture for our launch.

Cat's phone buzzed, then she let out a shriek. The launch video was ready from the editor. She hit play.

We huddled around her screen. Each scene pulsed with the story we'd been trying to tell. When the final drone shot of me running along the edge of the mountain faded and the Edge Theory Labs logo appeared, no one spoke. We just savored the goosebumps with tears welling in all three of our eyes.

At 1:04 a.m. on March 31, we pushed the site live. There was no fanfare, simply a quiet click and a collective breath. It felt less like launching a business and more like stepping off a cliff and trusting the wings we'd built would hold. *Would anyone actually buy this thing?* The question lingered, but I was too tired to entertain it and too proud that we'd made it to this point: the beginning.

After a few hours of restless sleep, I stopped by a café on my way to meet Rob before setting up our tub at Ironman Oceanside. My body was tired, but my mind was buzzing. As I waited in line, a sharp *cha-ching* broke through the morning sounds of the coffee shop. I didn't think it was my phone because I had never heard it make that sound before. But I pulled it out anyway and stared at the screen:

New Shopify Order! Tucker, $4,200 – 1 Edge Tub.

I froze. Then laughed out loud. People turned but I didn't care. I stepped out of line and headed straight to Rob's, suddenly wide awake. I didn't need coffee anymore. This drug was better than caffeine.

We made our way to the Ironman Village and set up our modest 10x10 booth. We rolled out the prototype carefully, like we were placing a sacred artifact on display. The irony of our sole $10,000 prototype surrounded by a $35 banner we had printed with our brand logo three days ago, and an $88 Amazon pop-up tent was not lost on us. People began to trickle in—some curious, some skeptical, most with no idea what they were looking at.

"What is this? A cold tub? Like, cold *air*?"

We smiled. "Think of it like an ice bath without the ice. Always cold, always clean. It can even turn into a hot tub."

We noticed how people responded and learned how to pitch it, refining our delivery with every interaction. And when the price point of $5,000 came up, some nodded, thinking it was a great deal; others looked at us like we had lost our minds. By the late afternoon, our energy started to fade as the crowd thinned. Doubt started to creep in. We sat quietly for a moment before I turned to Rob.

"We didn't come this far to only come this far."

He nodded. Just then, a man and his wife walked up. I launched into the story, walked them through the product, and answered every question. Rob peeled off to grab us a coffee, trusting I had it covered, and it seemed this interaction would be more of the same.

The man listened, nodding slowly. Then said, "Alright. I want one. Will you guys help me set it up when it's ready?"

"Absolutely," I said. "We've got you."

Then he said the four best words you can ask a salesperson. "Do you take AMEX?"

My heart jumped. We hadn't planned on taking orders in person—but I wasn't letting this one walk. I pulled up our site, ran through the bulky checkout process on my phone, and entered his details while he read them aloud. I clicked the *Submit Order* button and watched the wheel dial spin; with every revolution, more sweat accumulated on my palms. I held my breath.

Confirmation.

"You're good," I said with a grin, exhaling. "Welcome to the Edge Family!"

He walked away, stoked. Just then, Rob returned, holding two coffees.

"We got one!" I told him.

He blinked. "No way."

We laughed, high-fived, hugged. Two sales. Two days. Nearly $10,000. And there wasn't even a product to take home yet. And the best part was that the second sale was a complete stranger.

We sat on the curb drinking coffee, which now felt redundant, with the spring sun warming our backs. My head was spinning, heart thumping, and possibilities starting to open.

"If we sell one a day, thirty a month…" we joked, "we're millionaires."

What started as a wild idea in a garage was now standing on its own two feet.

And for the first time, it didn't feel like a dream anymore.

It was real.

It had begun.

CHAPTER 15

Fifty Tubs and a Dream

WE WERE OFF TO THE RACES. That first month was a blur of movement filled with early morning drives, weekend events, and demo setups in gym parking lots and trailheads before sunrise. Rob and I said yes to everything. If someone showed interest, we found a way to get a tub in front of them. At one point, we joked that we were chasing more marathons than the runners themselves.

It was gritty, unglamorous work. We hauled chillers in and out of vans, filled and drained tubs, explained cold therapy to skeptical passersby, and became pros at coiling extension cords and stiff hoses. But something happened when we got people in the water. They emerged with eyes wide and electrified, like I felt in Iceland.

On top of the recovery benefits, the look of clarity and empowerment on the faces of those meeting their edge became our north star. We knew that if we could deliver that to people, the sales would follow. So our unofficial strategy became "asses in tubs." Inelegant, but effective.

By the end of April, we had sold eight tubs. It was a start, and enough to keep us believing we might actually sell out our first fifty-unit inventory by the end of the year, which became our big goal. On social media, our momentum was building. People started tagging us, reposting plunges, and reaching out with curiosity since our tub was the first of its kind to the market and seemed to be solving a major pain point.

One afternoon, I heard the soft cha-ching from the Shopify app that I'd come to love. An order from someone none of us knew. He'd come through Instagram and placed the order without talking to me or Rob. Even more shocking, he bought the tub without seeing it in person, something we didn't think would ever be possible. And for the first time, I saw a business that could move without us holding its hand. We leaned into that energy, doubling down on content, storytelling, and digital strategy. In May, we nearly doubled April's numbers and sold fourteen tubs. Still modest, but growing brick by brick.

At the time, we had only three prototypes, still waiting for our first batch of production units. We guarded those prototypes like treasure, but there was one person we knew we wanted to gift one to: Mike Posner. After Doug Evans connected us to his team, I told them I didn't want anything in return. I just wanted to offer him a tub as a thank-you for his story, his music, and the way his path helped shape mine.

He said *yes*. A few days later, we drove up to LA and pulled into his driveway. Mike met us outside barefoot, shirtless, and seemingly stripped of ego. "Hey, man," he said softly, looking at the tub. "This thing is awesome," his smile inflected the last part of the word.

Within minutes, we were deep in conversation about Wim Hof, breathwork, research, transformation, and how Mike had evolved into a big influencer in the health and wellness space. Then, without fanfare, he stepped into the tub, opened TikTok, and went live. Mid-plunge, he invited me to talk to his thousands of fans watching live. I managed to get our pitch out, trying not to overthink the surreal moment.

Afterward, my phone lit up with messages. "Dude, I just saw you on Posner's live."

Mike stepped out surging with adrenaline and stoke. He invited us to take a dip next, which of course we did. Mike put his number in my phone and told me to keep him posted when we officially launch and to let him know how he could help. I got the chance to tell him how much his music and his story meant to me, and he received it fully and with sincere gratitude, as if it was the first time anyone had expressed anything like that to him.

On the drive home from LA, my heart felt still and full. The windows were down, the road stretched ahead, and neither of us spoke. The silence said everything. This success wasn't about a celebrity post or marketing lift; it felt much deeper. The one person I'd quietly hoped to meet was now in our tub, sharing it with the world, without us asking.

Rob broke the silence by turning to me and saying, "We might actually smash the preorder goal. What if we shoot for a hundred tubs by year's end?" He paused, then added with quiet conviction, "We didn't come this far to only come this far." He already knew I was in.

That moment stuck with me. It reinforced something I was starting to learn: when you give freely, without expectation, people feel it. The trust it builds accomplishes more than any pitch ever could. That energy opened more doors than we could've planned for.

By June, I launched virtual demos from my balcony, giving people the opportunity to book a call with me from the website. I would walk them through the tub on my apartment balcony over a Zoom call. I focused less on specs and more on what the cold could do for them. The calls started converting. One day, I closed five sales in a row. That pushed us over the line: fifty tubs, sold out. *Over $100,000 in revenue.* We cracked a nut in three months that most companies never get to. We had proof of concept for a product that the market wanted.

With this milestone, I felt it was time to move on from High Impact Coaching and put my full-time energy into Edge. Even with momentum on our side, I felt the tension rising. Leaving High Impact Coaching wasn't just about leaving a job. It meant letting go of stability, a steady paycheck, and five years of building something meaningful with people I cared about. Fear made itself known. *What if Edge doesn't work? What if we can't get it to the place where it can pay us?*

But beneath that noise, that quieter voice of purpose kept returning. It reminded me that I had to see this through. That I didn't come this far to stop at the edge. And thankfully, though I had hesitations, Zander didn't.

"Dude, I love you," he said, "but you've gotta go do this."

Jumping felt scary. Around that time, I started working with a mindset coach and mentor named Giorgio Genaus. He was my secret weapon—a real-life wizard who, among many other things, helped me navigate getting out of debt after I'd picked up bad spending habits and a poor relationship with money during my early high-income sales days.

Calm, intuitive, and armed with an Australian accent that made his wisdom sound even wiser, Giorgio had a way of holding space that helped me move through my biggest fears, doubts, and challenges. He reminded me that I wasn't really jumping off a cliff. I'd built a bridge by saving up, preparing, and creating a six-month runway for myself.

People love the idea of burning the boats, but I think that story is over-glorified. Not every act of courage needs to look like destruction. I didn't leap blindly. I built slowly, step by step, until the path forward felt sturdy enough to carry me, until the next breadcrumb was within reach. We live in a culture obsessed with all-or-nothing moves—the overnight success, the viral moment, the leap of faith with no safety net. But real transformation rarely works that way. It's less about explosion, more about evolution. Drops in the bucket that eventually overflow.

Courage, I realized, isn't just in the leap; it's in the building. It's in the discipline to prepare, the patience to wait, and the faith to keep planting seeds before you can see the harvest. Because sometimes the bravest thing you can do isn't to jump, it's to build the bridge.

By July 1, Rob and I were both full-time. We still hadn't taken a paycheck—aside from the burritos we indulged ourselves after closing a sale, which was more than enough for now.

As we both stepped in fully, it felt like bliss. There was a sense of possibility in the air, a current of potential carrying us through each day. Sales were rolling in, and people were saying *yes*—before we'd shipped a single tub. We were selling belief, and early adopters were giving us the one thing we needed most: time. Because they were paying in full up front and patiently waiting for the delivery date, that trust gave us room to bootstrap, using each sale to fund additional inventory purchases.

Momentum kept building. National Hockey League MVP Auston Matthews sent us a direct message. Ultimate Fighting Champion Brandon Moreno reached out. Then, Kyle from The Nelk Boys. And through a mutual contact, Dana White of the UFC came calling.

"Hey Josh, I love the tubs, buddy, these things are bad-ass. I want to get ten for my son's football team." Dana said sharply to the point.

"We can help you with that," I said, smiling.

Fifty grand hit our account that night.

It was that kind of summer. Every door that opened seemed to swing wide. And on top of it all, Rob got married. We were at our family's lake house in upstate New York, where I officiated the ceremony. Standing on the dock in matching suits, our inside pockets were stitched with the words: *Go All In* pressing against our hearts. Life felt rich. Sales were coming in while we slept.

But production was lagging. Our first fifty tubs were delayed. The shipment we thought would ship in July was now expected in late August. And then came a more serious issue. A small design flaw in the tub's hose connection—barely noticeable—was cracking and causing leaks during repeated setups. The flaw would eventually lead to total failure.

We hustled to find a fix, employing help from overseas engineers and even my crafty Aunt Debbie, who aided us immensely during the prototype phase. Rob finally found the fix, but it wasn't pretty. We could cut off the threads on each valve and rebuild them by hand using PVC fittings and heavy-duty cement. He stayed back in San Diego, gluing them together himself, while I went to the East Coast chasing down partnerships and sales, my days a blur of flights, hotel gyms, and meetings.

And another breadcrumb was waiting. I'd been following Jesse Itzler ever since reading his book *Living With a SEAL*. I admired his energy, his mix of hustle and humor, and thought, *One day, we'll get him a tub.*

That spark ignited when I saw his Instagram Story—Jesse and his crew squeezing a bulky ice bath into a van for their road trip. I'd messaged him before with no luck. But one guy in the van was Todd Anderson, a Michigan State alum like my dad. I messaged him: "Sparty on! We need to get you a better tub. Have you seen @edgetheorylabs?"

He replied right away: "Looks sick. Tell me more." A few voice notes later, he looped in Jesse's assistant. Next thing I knew, I was on the phone with her coordinating a visit that week since he happened to be at his home in Connecticut, and

I happened to be just a few hours' drive away in New York. I thanked Todd, who would become a good friend and investor.

I pulled up to Jesse's home, the lake breeze cutting through the trees. I was escorted to the back deck, and there he was. Jesse, sitting cross-legged on the porch, barefoot, playing a board game with his wife, Sara Blakely—self-made billionaire, Spanx founder, Shark Tank guest, and, as it turned out, just as sharp in person as she was on camera.

"Joshua," Jesse called out with a grin when I stepped around the corner. "Welcome, buddy. Come sit. I'm just about to finish kicking my wife's butt."

"Like hell you are," she shot back without missing a beat.

I laughed and eased into the moment, already feeling like part of the family. When the game ended, Jesse won, and Sara did not take it lightly. They both stood, gave me a hug, and welcomed me in. Then, they called for their kids. Each one came from a different corner of the property, each with a nanny in tow, and they gathered around the table.

"Kids," Jesse said, "come here. I want you to meet Joshua and hear about his company."

His family reminded me of how I'd been raised—minus the personal nannies—sitting in on my parents' conversations with curious strangers, learning from whoever passed through. Only this time, I got to be the stranger coming through the home with a story. Jesse looked at me and said with a half-smile, "No pressure, you're just pitching in front of a Shark."

I stayed cool, calm, and collected, told my story clearly, and walked them through the product. They listened closely. Asked thoughtful questions. Jesse leaned in.

"Well," he asked, "do you have one with you?"

"Yes, of course," I said, without hesitating. "It's in the trunk of my rental car."

"Let's fire that puppy up," he said, already on his feet. "I'll turn on the sauna."

Sara stood up and waved us off. "You boys have fun," she said before disappearing back into the house.

So that's what we did. For the next four hours, Jesse and I bounced between the sauna and the tub, trading stories, sweating, freezing, laughing. I asked him about his life, his philosophy, and the decisions that shaped him. He was generous, open, and game to go deep. By the end of the afternoon, he offered to buy a tub, but more than that, he posted about us on Instagram—a casual share that triggered a flood: thousands of new followers and a wave of new buyers. The experience was surreal. This thing we had built, this idea we had fought for, was now being handed off like a spark from one fire igniting the next.

When I drove toward the airport, ready to head home after this East Coast summer of sales, I felt something unfamiliar and undeniable settle in my chest. It was working. The same quiet force I'd followed throughout my life was undeniably showing up in the business. The Universe was partnering with us, laying down cosmic breadcrumbs and cracking open doors we couldn't have forced if we tried. And because we were moving *with* it, not *against* it, the path seemed to rise to meet our steps.

When I flew back from the East Coast, the first place I went was Rob's garage—though calling it a garage didn't quite fit anymore. It looked more like a makeshift production lab than any place that had ever housed a car. Fans stirred the air in the corners, tables were cluttered with half-assembled tubs, heavy metal blasted from an old speaker, and the smell of PVC glue clung to everything. Rob stood in the middle of it all with a gas mask on, shirt damp with sweat, hair a mess, fully immersed in the work and looking like a mad scientist.

He was deep into retrofitting the first fifty tubs, each requiring the same painstaking process: unpacking, unfolding, cutting the PVC threads off, gluing new parts by hand, holding them steady while the cement set, waiting an hour for it to cure, then repacking the tub like nothing had ever been touched. Every unit took time, focus, and patience.

We physically handled each one of the first 300 units before they left our inventory. We cut, glued, boxed, and sealed them ourselves. This wasn't the glossy side of entrepreneurship. It was long hours, sore backs, glue-caked fingers, and a garage that smelled like a hardware store and looked like a shipping center running on full throttle.

Just as we finished making space in the garage, the chillers arrived. To close those early sales, we'd promised local customers full delivery and setup. So we rented a U-Haul, loaded it to the ceiling, and began a scrappy tour across Southern California, showing up on doorsteps with our product and feeling like a cross between traveling salesmen and glorified pool boys.

Momentum kept building. August surpassed July in sales, but then came a deal that changed everything. A major wellness brand we'd been talking to pulled the trigger on a private-label order—custom tubs, their branding, our design. The invoice was for $250,000. Neither of us let ourselves believe it would happen until the wire cleared, but when it did, we just stood there in Rob's garage, surrounded by boxes, glue, and fan noise, staring at the number in our bank account. It still didn't feel real at first. After all the sweat, fumes, and midnight delivery runs, it was almost hard to believe how far we had come so quickly.

I looked at Rob, who still had PVC dust on his hands, and said what we were both already thinking. "Time for us to find an office space."

CHAPTER 16

With a Little Help from My Friends

The summer rush didn't let up. Labor Day marked our first big e-commerce holiday, and without running a single promotion, we moved more inventory in a week than we had projected for the entire month.

The spike in orders was thrilling—but it also stretched us thin. We were scrambling to keep up, increasing our next manufacturing batch from fifty to one hundred, then one-fifty, then two hundred. The real challenge wasn't selling people on cold therapy or justifying a $5,000 price tag. It was managing expectations. We were asking customers to wait up to ten weeks to receive their tub. Still, they said *yes*.

That weekend, I flew to Costa Rica for Ryland's bachelor party. We stayed in a villa tucked in the jungle with ten bedrooms, an infinity pool, and an ocean view that looked like a painting. I did my best to unplug—to surf, celebrate, and soak in the moment—but my phone buzzed nonstop with new orders. I'd glance down from the balcony between laughs and beers to see another sale come through. Watching the business grow from a jungle in Central America felt surreal.

One humid afternoon, Chad and I sat on the patio, listening to birds chatter through the trees and the surf breaking below.

"This thing is really taking off," he said, half in awe.

"Yeah, man," I nodded. "I'm gonna need some help soon."

He didn't flinch. "You just tell me where and when."

A few months earlier, Chad had been laid off. When he called to tell me the news, his voice carried lightness instead of frustration. "Honestly," he said, "I think it's a blessing. I feel like God's got something better lined up." That's classic Chad. Calm, faithful, and all-in. Since then, he had been doing some part-time sales here and there but was looking to sink his teeth into something more fulfilling.

One night, as we looked out over the jungle, he made an offer. "You're swamped. Let me take some sales calls off your plate. No need for a salary, just commission on what I close. I know I can sell this thing." Chad was a believer in cold immersion as it helped him heal and stay active after back surgery in his early twenties.

His help was exactly what I needed.

Back in San Diego, Rob and I toured one potential office space—and only one. It had everything: front office, break room, tall ceilings, built-in shelving, and a roll-up door that let in sunlight and views of palm trees. It sat a few blocks from the beach in Carlsbad, right off the freeway, minutes from both our homes. We didn't need to see another option. A vision snapped into place the moment we stepped inside.

We pictured tubs lined up along the walls, a sauna in the corner, a space to train, to work, to build a team. When the lease offer was accepted, we hit our signature handshake, pulled each other into a hug, and laughed like two kids who had talked their way into mischief they had no business being a part of.

We picked up the keys that September, brought a bottle of champagne, and walked the space slowly, mapping out the future in our minds. Only months earlier, we'd spoken this vision aloud in a hot springs tub under desert stars. Now it stood in front of us, concrete and tangible. We had our first HQ.

Now it was time to build the team.

Cat was the obvious first hire. She was already operating like a full-time employee—hustling deadlines, guiding creatively, and lighting up every room she walked into. We offered her the Director of Marketing role, and before we could finish the sentence, she cut us off with a grin and a "hell yes." She let go of her freelance clients, and we matched her income so she could go all in. Nikita also stepped in part-time from High Impact Coaching to help us with our organization and systems as we grew and I pulled in Laura who I had worked with in the past for some part time virtual administration work.

That fall, the warehouse became a revolving door of U-Hauls. Each tub needed Rob's valve fix before it could ship, and we needed hands. Doug Beckman didn't flinch. Doug had been a big brother figure to us ever since the unforgettable "wine opener night" in LA. He wasn't a startup guy by title, but he was in spirit. He showed up every day, ready to work—cutting valves, packing boxes, loading trucks. He didn't need glory. He just wanted to build something real with good people.

We also needed boots on the ground—someone who could run demos and activations so Rob and I could focus on the business. "Asses in tubs" was still our conversion strategy, and Rob and I couldn't keep burning half a day for a sale. So, I asked the Universe for help to bring someone to us.

A few days later, on a sales call with a college soccer coach, we wrapped up the conversation, and he paused.

"This is random," he said, "but my sister's moving to SoCal. She's super sharp, athletic, and I think you guys would get along well. Are you hiring by chance?"

"Put us in touch," I said.

One call with me, one with Rob, and she was hired.

By October, Chad was fully trained and closing deals with ease. And he didn't stop. Sale after sale, he brought his warmth, focus, and follow-through. We offered him a part-time role with a small base plus commission. That felt right for both of us. And for the first time, I had someone I trusted to run with sales, which gave me space to pull back from the daily grind and start thinking further out. The business was growing. And so were we.

Then Sam arrived.

Tall, dark-haired, with perfect posture and a grounded presence that commanded attention, Sam was already a legend in the Wim Hof world, being one of the earliest certified instructors in North America. That summer, he booked a call with me, curious about the tub, and we clicked immediately.

He showed up to our first in-person meeting on his bike. He'd ridden twenty miles just to check it out. As I walked him through the setup, the conversation naturally deepened. We connected over the integrity behind the practice. We shared the same frustration with how performative the space had become, with too much flash and not enough depth. For both of us, this work wasn't about virality. It was about service, safety, science, and soul.

Sam had first seen me on Mike Posner's TikTok live. He'd met Mike earlier that year at Doug Evans' wedding, where the two of them had fallen into a long, winding conversation about cold immersion, breathwork, and transformation. We were each other's next cosmic breadcrumbs.

We gave Sam one of our first Marketing Fleet tubs—a pilot program we were just starting, in which we placed units with teachers, creators, and event leaders in exchange for content and visibility. But Sam didn't just take the tub and disappear. He helped shape the entire program, offered feedback, and leaned in as if he were already on the team. Eventually, he was. He became our Director of Performance and Coaching.

Bringing people in slowly had become a guiding principle. Crawl, walk, then run. Start with trust, test in real work, and build forward only when it makes sense. Start slow. Get to know each other inside the rhythm of the work. Date before you get married. Build off-ramps. Set expectations. Keep the communication clear, and take the working relationship one step at a time. The goal was never about going fast, but about going far. This principle has served me well, *especially* when working with friends.

November arrived, and as the year began to wind down, one more big reunion event for Ryland, Chad, Danny, and me was happening in the Florida Keys: Ryland's wedding. When I arrived, I was greeted by warm air, long shadows, and a sunset that scattered rays into the Gulf like gold coins. Ryland had asked me to officiate the wedding—an honor I didn't take lightly. During the ceremony, I told the story of how we met on the first day of college in Microbiology class, and how a simple wine opener changed everything.

The night before the wedding, we gathered barefoot on the beach, tiki torches flickering in the sand, metal handpan thumping low. The evening felt light and celebratory, but in my pocket I carried a secret I couldn't wait to deliver. Rob and I had decided that starting in December, we'd offer Chad a full-time role. And I wanted to deliver the news in person.

I find him, and we drift away from the group, down a quiet stretch of sand where the only light comes from the fire.

"Chad," I say, steadying my breath.

He looks up, sensing the shift. I don't draw it out.

"How would you feel about coming on full-time at Edge Theory Labs as our Head of Sales?"

He stands still, taking it in. Then his face breaks into a grin that goes deeper than joy.

"I'd say it would be an honor," he says, voice catching slightly, "and a God-damn privilege, brother."

We shake hands, then pull into a hug. From two kids in the basement of our fraternity house, we find ourselves here, ready to build something we believe in, together.

Before I could linger too much in the warmth of this wave, the next wave crashed in. The balance returned.

That weekend, a text came in from a pro hockey player who owned one of our first tubs. "Hey man, it's not working anymore."

At first, I thought it was a one-off. We'd had a few issues—small things, usually fixed with a phone call or a quick video message. But as the second wave of production units rolled out, the messages started to multiply. Slowly, then steadily.

The pattern became clear: certain parts weren't holding up, and chillers stopped running. The vacuum pump, in particular, was failing under regular use. We flagged it with our manufacturer and immediately began upgrading parts for future production runs. This kind of refinement was expected for a first-gen hardware product, but we hadn't adequately accounted for the customer service load and expenses that we'd need to front to manage it. It wasn't just a few scattered calls; it was a steady stream. And we needed to build a system, a team, and a plan around it.

Rob jumped in first, fielding every message, walking customers through fixes, and when a solution wasn't possible, we agreed on a simple rule: replace the unit. No questions asked. Everyone was still under warranty, and we had enough margin to stand behind what we sold. As the tickets piled up, Rob handed the baton to Doug, who took over the inbox and phone line with the same grounded, no-ego attitude he brought to everything else.

That helped. But a thorn had already started to take root. Each text I got from someone with an issue sank my heart. The sales momentum was still strong, but in the quiet moments, doubt started to whisper. *What if more units fail? What if this gets worse?*

Then came more manufacturing delays.

Production issues hit again, and suddenly, customers who had already waited ten weeks—the longest we'd promised—were now facing another two or three. It wasn't our fault, not directly. But we felt responsible. These people had trusted us and had waited patiently. It felt like a cop-out to simply send out a mass email notifying them of further delays and hold our breath, hoping they didn't want a refund. So I decided to own it.

I pulled a report: seventy-six customers had already passed the ten-week mark. I cleared my calendar and called each one of them. One by one. I let them know what was happening, apologized, and offered either a free accessory or a partial refund—something small, but human.

Most people were shocked that a founder would take the time to reach out personally. They thanked me. They stayed on board. Only one person out of the seventy-six asked for a refund, giving me a great lesson on what good can come from sticking your nose in the mud and facing a challenge like that head-on.

But it wasn't the calls that wore me down. It was everything else.

The high of summer—the surge of sales, the buzz of growth—had faded into the deeper weight of what we were building. We weren't just a couple of guys chasing runners through gym parking lots anymore. We were a real company. Something we wanted, no doubt, but the responsibility had increased. We had a team to pay. Customers to support. Suppliers we depended on. Orders to fulfill. Valves to fix. Overflowing inboxes to clear. Finances to manage. Schedules to plow through. Logistics breaking down.

Every win now came with a shadow. Every decision carried more weight.

And somewhere in all that noise, I could feel a shift. The next season of the business had already begun.

CHAPTER 17

From Castle to Kingdom

That fall's freedom—when everything still felt like play and possibility—had begun to harden. The dream was working and the business was growing, but it no longer felt light. The pressure was starting to fray my edges. Sleep came in fragments. My body was tight, my thoughts cluttered. I could feel fear rising in the back of my mind, and I was trying to distract myself from it.

A friend had introduced me to Christina Rice, known as Christina The Channel, who is a gifted energy healer and intuitive channel. She was my age, soft-spoken, yet she moved with quiet confidence. She had short blonde hair and big bright eyes that told me she saw things.

I showed up at her home for an energy-healing session with an open mind and the hope that I'd leave feeling different than when I arrived. She lived alone in a four-bedroom home in a clean, quiet neighborhood, and her Mercedes G-Wagon was parked out front. Clearly, she was not your typical late-twenties woo-woo healer. She welcomed me in and walked me upstairs to what felt more like a portal than a spare room.

The scent of burning sage curls through the air as I step barefoot into the healing room. My energy shifted the moment I crossed the threshold—like walking through a membrane, from noise into stillness. The walls were soft white, dappled with crystals and subtle symbols. Light filtered through gauzy curtains, catching the smoke in a slow dance. Lying back on the table with the cotton sheet cool beneath me, I closed my eyes.

For the next hour, she worked. I couldn't see what she was doing, couldn't explain it if I tried, but I could feel it—like something inside me being gently cleared, rearranged. It was almost like she was performing energetic surgery, without physically touching me, just hands hovering and moving above my body.

Afterwards, she handed me a cup of tea and sat with me. That's when the session really began.

She started speaking calmly and with focus, as if she were reading a book. She told me where I was leaking energy, which chakras were blocked. She told me things about myself I hadn't said aloud. I nodded, stunned, more than once.

And then she said something that caught me completely off guard.

"I also did some healing on your business."

"My business?" I questioned back. Raising an eyebrow, half curious, half guarded.

"Yeah, most founders don't know it, but your business is its own entity."

I laughed. "Yeah, you mean, like our legal structure? We're a Delaware C Corp."

She smiled. "No, not like that. Your business is its own *energetic* entity. It's alive. It has its own soul. Most founders don't honor this. They try to force their business to become what *they* want, instead of listening to what it's actually here to be. Like a parent trying to force their kid into piano lessons when they really are here to play the violin."

That resonated deeply.

"So... how's it doing?" I asked, almost sheepishly.

She looked right at me. "It's beautiful. Strong and healthy. Edge Theory Labs feels like a glowing white castle."

I felt a wave of relief wash over me. We were doing something right.

"But," she said, pausing before I could get too proud, "it doesn't want to be a castle. It wants to be a kingdom. You need to think bigger."

Think bigger? I thought. *We have just shattered every goal we thought was a stretch. Hit $2 million in sales. Built an office, a team, received celebrity endorsements, and here she was having the audacity to tell me to think bigger?*

I drove home quietly that night, headlights cutting through the dark, wondering what a kingdom might look like. Wondering if I had the courage to find out.

As January unfolded and the dust of our first full year began to settle, I saw the road ahead with a very different lens than the year before. We had crossed the starting line, but now we were deep in the race, no longer trying to build momentum, but managing it. The noise was louder, the stakes higher, the terrain unknown.

Rob and I sat down with our whiteboards, notebooks, and overly strong coffee to map out 2023. We gave ourselves permission to think bigger. Not just more sales, but more impact. What would it look like to transform 1,000 lives by selling 1,000 tubs? That meant no half-measures. It meant aiming for a $5 million year. The goal was both bold and audacious, but not unthinkable.

To align the team, we planned a Team Development Day. Everyone together, in one room, to talk about who we were becoming and how we'd get there. We pushed together couches and mismatched chairs, wheeled in the whiteboard, rigged up our big TV, and turned our humble flex warehouse space into a summit hall. It felt both makeshift and magical, like building a blanket fort with friends. We set up next to the new eight-person sauna that had just arrived; the cedar still smelled fresh. Fresh, like this new year, filled with promise, it stood like a monument to the kind of culture we were building.

One of our first exercises as a team was to name our community. Our Edge Tubs were catching on fast, but "Edge Users" sounded sterile. "Edgers" had a weird innuendo sort of energy. We opened the floor for ideas. Chad raised his hand first, like he had the obvious answer to the equation the teacher just scribbled on the whiteboard.

"What if we called them *Ledgends*? Like legends, but with Edge in it."

A pause.

Doug, from across the room, deadpanned, "There's no D in legends, bro." Then he cracked up; the entire room followed.

Chad laughed too, "Right. Good catch. Never mind, carry on!"

Spelling was never one of Chad's strong suits, but I wrote it on the board anyway: *Ledgends*. After the rest of the suggestions, we all circled back to Ledgend. Something about it stuck. It felt gritty, bold, unique, and a little weird—like us. So we inked it.

LEDGEND *(n)*
ledg·end /'lejənd/
Someone who is committed to finding their edge, stepping beyond their comfort zone, and pushing the limits of possibility to unlock their greatest human potential.

That was it.

Rob and I then pulled up a new mission and vision statement and presented it to the team, along with our team philosophy, hoping it would resonate.

Mission Statement
At Edge Theory Labs, we believe that greatness happens at the edge of your comfort zone.

We're on a mission to give you the tools that give you the edge. The edge on recovery, on performance, on winning the day.

Whatever goals you are striving towards, whatever greatness you aspire to achieve, keep going. You got this, and we got you.

Go All In!

Vision Statement
Our vision is to build a company that goes beyond just selling a product to make money, but rather innovates solutions that make people healthier and give them the opportunity to be part of a community of like-minded high performers. We envision Edge Theory Labs as the leader in the recovery market, providing recovery solutions in multiple verticals. As a result, we are empowering people to stress less and achieve more, develop a deeper relationship with themselves, and unlock their maximum human potential.

The Edge Philosophy
At Edge Theory Labs, we believe people are at the heart of everything we do—our customers, affiliates, ambassadors, partners, and most importantly, our team. By treating people with dignity and respect, we build a foundation for our Mission and Vision to thrive. Doing what's right for our people won't always be easy, but that challenge is what sets us apart.

Startups attract people for a reason: the chance to create real impact, grow fast, work with those who value your voice, and help build something meaningful. Many companies miss this, leading to disconnection and dysfunction. At the core of it all is trust. No one asks for *less* trust—yet most corporate systems are designed to limit it. We choose differently. At Edge Theory Labs, we commit to trusting our team and honoring the reasons you chose to join us.

We set a high bar—for ourselves, for each other, and for what we're building. We are a team first, and being on this team is a privilege. Being "all in" means collaborating well, making smart, timely decisions, speaking up when problems arise, and staying focused on the highest-leverage work. We want our team to wake up refreshed and excited to tackle the day's challenges.

And yes, we want to enjoy the ride. Work should be an extension of life—not the other way around. We promote flexibility to fully experience life's moments. We support each other in chasing big goals and believe work should never come at the cost of health. In fact, we celebrate wellness through movement, athleticism, and, naturally, plenty of cold plunges.

The day continued with open-hearted shares, clear vision, and deep alignment. We closed, of course, with a breathwork session, then fire and ice: sauna rounds, cold plunges, music bumping, laughter echoing off cinderblock walls.

This company wasn't just about our product anymore. It was about people. About a culture we were building together, one breath, one joke, and one brave moment at a time.

We were redefining what it meant to *work together*. And I knew we were doing something right when Cat burst through the doors one morning later that week—despite having planned to work from home—and yelled, "I had FOMO not being here!" That kind of energy can't be faked.

I had made a point of creating a unique handshake with each team member. Not because I wanted to be the cool boss with an NBA tunnel intro, though I won't lie, that was part of it. But because I wanted each person to be greeted in a way that was just *ours*. A ritual, a reminder that they were seen as individuals. Culture, I came to find, isn't created by memos. It's created by moments.

That afternoon of the Team Development Day, we launched the *Misogi Fund*. Inspired by Jesse Itzler's idea, it's built on the belief that once a year, you should do something so hard and uncertain there's a fifty/fifty chance you'll fail. After experiencing firsthand how retreats like Iceland and Mt. Shasta, and endurance races shaped me, we didn't just want to encourage our team to experience transformative challenges—we wanted to fund one such experience each year.

After everyone departed, Rob and I remained to stack up the folding chairs and restore relative order to the chaos of the room after our first Team Development Day. In a moment of inspiration and recognition that leaders do, in fact, go first, I turned to Rob and said, "I'm cashing in that IOU."

He looked at me. "What IOU?"

"The Ironman one."

He raised his eyebrows, smiled, and nodded. "Oh yeah... that one."

"Think we're too busy?"

He laughed. "Of course we are."

I grinned. "Exactly. When has that ever stopped us? We'll do the half Ironman in March in San Diego as a tune-up, then Arizona for the full in November."

He paused, then gave the only acceptable answer.

"Screw it. I'm in."

That's when I knew the castle wasn't just standing idle; it was rising. Not as a monument to what we'd built, but as the foundation for who we were still becoming. I could still hear

Christina's words in the back of my mind: *This business isn't just a business. It is alive...* And I knew it would become a kingdom through the heartbeat of this team's culture and character. Through the Edge Philosophy lived out loud.

So we stepped into 2023—not knowing what was waiting for us, but ready to meet it.

CHAPTER 18

Order Up

THE YEAR 2023 BEGAN WITH ROCKET fuel. After gathering the team around our shared vision and setting the bold, maybe even ridiculous goal of transforming the lives of a thousand people, we entered the new year with momentum behind us and stars in our eyes.

The inbox became a battlefield of sorts, a mix of customer service land mines and treasure troves. One day, the Jonas Brothers were tagging us on Instagram, and another day, it was a frustrated customer. Pro athletes, wellness leaders, and influencers reached out like we were the new kid everyone wanted to know.

Some days felt surreal. Like when I found myself with Dana White in his private office at UFC in Las Vegas toasting a shot of whiskey with Conor McGregor and Bruce Buffer. Other days felt like a grind. Getting on the next flight to fly across the country to fix a unit and save a major partnership. The high of growth never completely faded, but behind the scenes, customer service issues were stacking up. We were patching things up, trusting our future selves and our manufacturer to figure it out. But we hadn't yet addressed the deeper problems.

When spring arrived, Ironman training kicked off. My goal this time was to make it to the start line. If I showed up with a steady mind and a healthy body, I knew I'd finish. This time, I trained with consistency rather than obsession. Rob and I logged long hours working, training, and then recovering at the office in the stillness of the ice or the heat of the cedar sauna, continuously dreaming bigger. These quiet moments are etched deepest in my memory.

By then, the team had grown to twelve. A dozen personalities, passions, and talents coming together. We were building fast. And still, in many ways, we felt like beginners.

In early 2023, I sat down with Cat for our weekly one-on-one in the Summit Room. The name had started as a joke, but stuck. It was the glass-walled meeting room near the front of the office, always faintly scented with coffee and dry-erase markers. Rob had just brewed his fresh afternoon pot, which he did like clockwork after lunch every day. Cat walked in ready to jam.

"Two things," she said, flipping open her notebook. "First, we need to redo the website. It's fine, but we can increase conversion. Same with email marketing. There's a lot of untapped growth there."

"Agreed," I said. "Let's find a copywriter. Someone who can do email, but can also own the strategy and execution of our messaging."

"You know anyone?"

"I don't think so," I say, racking my brain. "But now that we're looking, I know the right person will show up. Let's add it to our order from the Universe."

She nodded like it was already done. "Second thing—paid ads. It's time. Finding a good agency is hard, but I think a little gas could take this thing to another level."

She was right. Until now, we'd built everything organically through partnerships, word of mouth, and social content.

That approach gave us a strong foundation, but we were ready to grow.

"We need a partner who understands high-ticket hardware," I said. "This isn't just another product on a shelf."

"For sure," she said. "So, is it too late to add it to our Universe order?"

She grinned. I mimed hitting a kitchen bell.

"Order up."

We laughed, then let it go. Fully trusting that the right person, the right agency, the right path was already on its way.

Because that's the thing about cosmic breadcrumbs, they're not just waiting to be found. They're finding you, too. What if everything you desire actually desires you even more? What if all you're seeking has been seeking you all along?

Our copywriter showed up later that week. Literally.

In our small Carlsbad office park, I was often spotted pacing barefoot outside during partnership calls, shirt off, soaking in the sun like some wild, tanned executive monk. That's just how I worked best. Rob and I had to eventually make a "shoes-and-shirt" rule to keep things professional, though we blamed all policies on our fictional HR rep, Harry Reid. However, the "wet zone"—where the tubs, sauna, and workout gear lived—was still fair game.

I had just come in from one of those sun-drenched strolls when the office door creaked open.

"Josh?" a voice called gently.

I turned—and couldn't believe my eyes. Standing there was Jake Heilbrunn—the same Jake who introduced me to Zander all those years ago. We hadn't talked in ages, but there he was, wide-eyed and smiling.

"Dude, Jake! What's up, brother!" I said, giving him a big, sweaty, bare-chested hug.

"This is the Edge office, huh? Wild," he said, glancing around. "I was just next door at the chiropractor."

He explained that his usual spot in Del Mar had been double-booked, so they sent him to the Carlsbad location. He'd never been there before. And, just as he was about to walk out the door, he saw what looked like a barefoot, shirtless version of me walking into the office next door.

We caught up for a few minutes, settling onto the couch near the front door.

"What are you up to these days?" I asked.

"I've been doing copywriting and email strategy for wellness brands," he said, smiling. "It's been amazing."

Of course he was. I pulled Cat in from the other room and introduced them. Jake walked out with an offer.

He got to work immediately—building our automated email flows and helping shape the brand's creative direction with Cat. And we saw an instant lift in revenue directly from Jake's efforts. The two of them quickly became a powerhouse duo, always huddled in the corner of the office, often mid-laugh and plotting something that ended with me freezing in an ice bath for content. Add in the swaggy videographer, Tyler AKA TyNelly, whom I had worked with before with Zander, and the brand leveled up fast. The storytelling sharpened, and the visuals came to life.

And then, right on cue, the ad agency showed up too—just after I stopped looking for them.

We'd put out feelers and reviewed a handful of proposals, but none felt right. Some were good but lacked relevant experience; others missed the vision entirely. I closed my laptop after rejecting another pitch and felt that familiar tightening in my chest—the signal I've learned to trust. When I feel that tightening, I realize I am forcing a square peg into a round hole. That resistance clearly reminds me that I'm trying to do more than my part. Whenever things start to feel forced, it's time for me to let go.

So I did. I surrendered the search and grabbed my duffel bag to head to my weekly basketball reset.

I laced up and started warming up when I noticed two familiar faces walk onto the court that I hadn't seen in months: Curt and Pat. We'd played plenty of games together in the past. They were intense, driven, and fun guys who played with their whole hearts and left it all on the court. Pat and I often found ourselves matched up against each other when we played, and I always loved that sense of competition. Iron sharpens iron, and we were iron for each other on the court. We didn't know each other beyond those weekly basketball games, but we shared a sincere mutual respect for one another.

"Pat, what happened?" I joked as he sank a warm-up jumper. "You finally had enough of me cooking you and needed a break?"

He laughed, catching the ball. "Yeah, right."

Then Curt chimed in. "Actually, we started an agency. We're running paid ads for brands."

I raised an eyebrow.

"Yeah," Pat added, "we just finished a campaign for a company that sells $2,000 air conditioning units, it totally crushed."

"Of course it did," I said, letting a three fly. Swish.

A few days later, they met with Cat. One conversation was all it took. She was in. We brought them on shortly after. The truth is, I already knew everything I needed to know about them by observing the way they played the game of basketball. You can fake a pitch deck, but you can't fake how you hustle back on defense after turning the ball over.

From day one, Curt and Pat delivered. Their results were jaw-dropping. At one point, we were seeing a 28x return on ad spend—unheard of in an industry where 2–5x is standard. This meant that for every dollar spent on ads, 28 dollars in sales came back to us. Even slow weeks returned well over average.

They were the first and only ad agency we ever hired.

With email and paid marketing firing on all cylinders, the spring of 2023 burst open like a flower catching full sun.

Our monthly revenue jumped from $300,000 to $800,000 almost overnight. The dream of selling one thousand tubs in a year no longer seemed bold—it felt inevitable. We might even double it.

With the pace picking up, Rob needed more support. He had been shouldering more of the operational weight, and we knew it was time to bring in someone who could own that lane. We needed a Director of Operations to build the systems, manage the chaos, and let him get back into his zone of genius. Thankfully, we didn't have to look far.

Back when we first launched, Rob and I had been accepted into the San Diego Sport Innovators accelerator program—four months of mentorship calls, support, and community. One of the mentors assigned to us was TJ. He was tall, soft-spoken, with a gentle confidence. A neatly kept combover and thick black-rimmed glasses gave him an understated professor vibe. He had built and eventually closed down a mountain biking apparel brand, and was now in a sort of liminal space, ready for what came next.

Rob had a full-blown bromance with him from day one. They spoke the same language—supply chains, product iterations, lean logistics. TJ had even taught himself Mandarin just so he could negotiate better with manufacturers in China. That alone made Rob's eyes light up like he'd seen a magic trick. We extended TJ an offer and he accepted.

Not long after we hired TJ, March 31st arrived, which marked exactly one year since the official launch of Edge Theory Labs. Our one-year anniversary fell on the same day as our half-Ironman in San Diego. This time, we weren't running the booth ourselves at the expo. Our team had it handled while we were running the race. And as I looked around, I saw what had taken shape. We had done millions in sales. We had an office that felt like home. We had people we believed in showing up every day to make this dream a reality.

Rob and I crossed the finish line together of that half-Ironman side by side, holding an Edge Theory Labs flag. But as I let the moment wash over me, my mind drifted toward the full Ironman still ahead of us in Arizona that fall. Redemption was coming, and I was ready.

That spring, a customer to whom Chad had sold a tub turned out to be the Director of Performance for the Los Angeles Clippers. He loved our product and loved us even more. A few weeks later, he introduced us to a league contact who ran the NBA Trainers Association.

"He thinks we can sell to every team in the league," Chad told me.

Next thing I know, we're on a flight to Chicago, heading to the NBA Trainers Association spring meeting to showcase our tub to every team in the league.

After checking into our hotel, Chad and I hunt down our massive tub shipment—which, of course, has been delivered to the wrong building. Tired, a little sweaty, and low on energy, we hit the hotel lobby mini-mart.

"Don't worry, I got this one," Chad says, grabbing trail mix and water. "You bought food at the airport."

I shake my head, laughing. "Chad, put it on the business card. This is a business trip."

He pauses. "Wait, really? You sure?"

"Chad," I say, still grinning, "The business is covering this because we're here to grow it. We have a budget for this kind of thing."

He nods slowly, like it's clicking in. "Man... the boss gives us a budget and everything."

We used to joke about "the boss" like he was some invisible man in a suit. The inside joke was cheeky and fun, but it also had a purpose. Everyone wants to be in charge, to "be their own boss"—another one of our culture's glorified obsessions. But honestly, that part is easy. The real work is learning how to be your own best employee. It means keeping promises to yourself, honoring deadlines that no one else enforces, and showing up with integrity even when the reward isn't immediate. The real question is simple: *Would you hire yourself?*

The next day, we set up our booth, pitched for hours, smiled until our cheeks hurt, then broke everything down with sore feet and full hearts. Over dinner that night, we could barely hold our heads up.

We've just sold eight units to NBA Teams. We sit in silence, not because there's nothing to say, but because sometimes gratitude doesn't need words.

I glance over. "College Josh and Chad in Room 004 of the Sig Ep basement would be *real* proud of us right now."

Chad nods, eyes misting. "Yeah, man. It's actually insane how much the Universe has our back. Like... pinch me. We're literally living our dream."

"You wanted to work in sports," I remind him. "Now you're doing deals with your favorite teams, shaking hands with coaches you used to watch on TV. And we're doing it together in a business that I'm running."

As if on cue, the bar speakers start playing *Pursuit of Happiness* by Kid Cudi—our anthem.

Chad looks like he might explode. "Tell me what you know about dreaming!" he shouts, practically ripping off his shirt in a signature Chad burst of joy that has actually destroyed more than a few shirts over the years.

I laugh, soaking it in. "I can't wait to see what's next."

When the check comes, he doesn't even flinch and lets me take it.

"Okay," he says, kicking back in his seat. "I'm starting to like business trips."

After that, we hit every major league trainers convention: the NFL in Vegas, the NHL in Phoenix, the MLB in Orlando. At each one, Chad and I showed up like kids in a candy store, wide-eyed, brains buzzing, fueled by the thrill of watching our dream take shape, one cosmic breadcrumb at a time.

I felt like the business was a mirror for my personal and spiritual development. All the principles I had spent years learning—trust, surrender, alignment, intuition—were no longer abstract lessons written in a journal. They were being forged into my daily experience. *Ask and you shall receive.* That part was working magically. The mirror kept delivering the right people, the right teachers, the right messages at just the right time.

But the mirror doesn't just show your best angles. It reveals the shadows too, the parts you'd rather not see, the truths you'd rather not admit. But by that point, I understood that growth rarely happens where we're comfortable. It hides in the places that ask more of us.

And I still had a lot more to see.

CHAPTER 19

The Growth You Asked For

THE BLOOMING OF SPRING QUICKLY GAVE way to summer heat. I flew to Wisconsin to officiate a close friend's wedding. I was becoming the go-to officiant for my friends' weddings, which was an honor that I infused with intention and storytelling. I was looking forward to this one, as it would be a welcome chance to exhale and reconnect. But before the welcome party had even started, my phone started lighting up.

Customer service issues flooded my DMs, texts, and inbox. Frustrated voices coming from all sides. I missed several calls from Doug, our Head of Customer Support. Doug doesn't call twice unless something's really wrong. After I checked into my hotel room, I called him back. His voice was tight and measured. I could tell he was doing his best to stay composed. Rob was supposed to be taking time off that week, finally taking his first real break since we'd launched, which meant I would be holding the wheel while he was unplugged at the lake.

Doug laid out the situation. We had an inventory problem, and it was worse than we realized. Normally, when a unit had issues, we could send a replacement to make it right. But our inventory had dried up while we were waiting for our next shipment of tubs because the volume of issues had spiked. We were replacing up to ten units a week.

We had a process for providing the best customer experience by replacing many of the chillers that had issues with refurbished units to minimize downtime for customers. The faulty ones coming back couldn't be refurbished by our repair team quickly enough to turn around as replacements, so they were stacking up in the warehouse. To make matters worse, we ran out of packing foam of all things. Without it, we couldn't even ship the repaired units. There was no more room to delay, no more buffer. We were at a standstill.

I stared at the hotel wall for a long moment. The late-afternoon light stretched itself across the beige curtains, warm and honeyed, like it was trying to soothe me. This was the unglamorous side of entrepreneurship that doesn't get shared online. This was the lonely, quiet part; the part that tests what you're really made of. I inhaled deeply, felt the air settle in my chest, then exhaled with purpose. The laptop waited like an old friend who knew what came next. I opened it and got to work.

Sitting on the edge of the bed in that small hotel room, I began outlining a new return-and-repair program. It wouldn't fix everything, but it could stop the bleeding and give us a path forward. I drafted the messaging, defined the process, and started hunting down short-term foam solutions—anything that would keep us moving.

The vast majority of our customers had no issues at all. But when you're dealing with thousands of people, small percentages still mean hundreds of problems, and thousands of emails and long phone calls to coordinate solutions. And it only takes one angry message, one legal threat, one person who's had enough, to make it all feel like it's teetering.

As I sat there working, three more messages came in. All urgent. All needed answers.

For a moment, I felt the urge to run. To disappear for a while and leave the mess behind. But I didn't. I stayed. I kept working through it. I remembered a lesson Dad taught me; this is what you do. And I remembered what my teacher, the cold, had taught me about embracing stress and facing it head-on.

I'm now late for the welcome party. My heart feels tight. I should be catching up with old friends, raising a glass, hugging people I haven't seen in six years. But instead, I'm buried in problems, holding everything together by a thread. Eventually, I reach a stopping point, not because everything is fixed, but because there's nothing more I can do in this moment. I close the laptop, exhale, rub my face, and get dressed.

This is when I discover one more problem: I've forgotten to pack socks.

All I have are flip-flops and frustration growing in the pit of my stomach. I need to find a store, which means missing even more of the evening's celebration. The irritation swells, a silent scream rising in my chest. But underneath the noisy thoughts comes the whisper I readily recognize. A quiet invitation in the form of the question: *What if this isn't happening to you, but for you?*

I slide into my rental car and pull onto the road. The last traces of daylight melt behind the hills, and dusk drapes itself across the landscape like a soft, indigo blanket. The lake shimmers with one final glint of sun, then fades into shadow as I head toward Sister Bay, a sleepy town with one blinking light and, if the Universe is on my side, a single pair of socks waiting for me.

Somewhere along that drive, I whisper a prayer. *Please show me you're with me. Please give me a sign I'm exactly where I need to be.*

I pull into the parking lot of a small, family-owned shop tucked between a coffee shop and a used bookstore. There's a hand-painted sign on the door and wind chimes hanging above the entrance. Inside, I smell a faint blend of cedar and lavender.

A mother and her teenage daughter glance up at me from behind the counter. Their kindness feels familiar, even though we are strangers to one another. The mom greets me and asks what I'm looking for.

"Dress socks," I say, laughing at myself. "Forgot to pack any."

"Oh, we've got you covered, sweetie," she says, motioning to a small wooden rack.

I let out a breath I didn't realize I was holding in.

They help me find a pair, and we start talking. At first, it's small talk—where I'm from, what brings me to town—but something about their presence slows me down. I find myself sharing more. About the wedding, the business, and my life in California, which they find fascinating. They tell me about their store, how long it's been in the family, how summer brings people from all over, but not many people from Cali.

Then I see it. The sign I had prayed for.

Painted behind the counter on a big wall is a mural of a tree, its branches stretched wide, its roots running deep. Nestled into the bark are the words: *"Unless you try to do something beyond what you have already mastered, you will never grow."*

I stop. My whole body absorbs this sign, clear as day, in a town I hadn't even heard of a week ago. I snapped a photo and set it as my phone wallpaper, which becomes my compass as I navigate the parts of the business I still haven't mastered, and the parts of myself I'm still discovering.

I asked for growth. And here it is. Not wrapped in ease, but in friction. What a privilege it is to be overwhelmed by a life I once prayed for. Even this customer service storm is a breadcrumb here for my growth, and it is just as sacred as the others along the way, like our copywriter Jake stumbling into our office at the perfect moment.

During the trip back from the wedding, I felt a quiet resolve settle inside me. The messy parts of the business, the ones we'd been sidestepping, were no longer hiding. Seeing them clearly was its own kind of relief. The pretending was over.

Rob and I leaned in, had the hard conversations, and rolled up our sleeves. Together we waded into the mess. I felt like we finally opened a cluttered closet that had been waiting for us, with stale air rushing out and half-forgotten things tumbling to the floor. But once we brought everything out into the light, we didn't feel so overwhelmed.

Not long after, we received the shipment we'd been counting on: two hundred chillers and tubs, finally released after sitting in customs at the Port of Long Beach for over a week. These units would help us fulfill orders still pending and replace faulty units from earlier batches. Just seeing them stacked in the warehouse brought a wave of relief.

But that sense of relief went by the wayside once we decided to pull a few units for testing, a habit we'd adopted after our previous shipment of one hundred units arrived with faulty vacuum pumps. That experience had left us scrambling, so we weren't going to be caught off guard again.

We pulled the first one for testing, and the touchscreen didn't work. So we pulled another one. Same thing. After our analysis, we determined that the screens weren't working on nearly half of the batch. But then came the worst news of all: the manufacturer had known. They told us it wasn't a big deal, that customers could still control the unit from the smartphone app. They'd shipped the units anyway without saying a word.

At that point, we weren't just dealing with a product issue—we had a trust issue, and that cut deeper than any technical failure. We did the only thing we could. We opened every box. We unwrapped each unit carefully, used a heat gun to loosen the adhesive on the screen overlay, manually replaced the screens, tested them ourselves, and then carefully reboxed every single unit. The work was painfully slow, tedious, and draining, but it had to be done.

Rob and I spent long nights sorting through what came next. The business was scaling fast—faster than our infrastructure could keep up. The ads were working almost too well. Orders were pouring in, but we were undercapitalized, which felt at times like sprinting up Mt. Everest in worn-out sneakers. We needed help. We needed to raise money so we could level up. We needed to build a Generation 2 unit with a new manufacturer.

Raising capital was a daunting task. The fundraising landscape in 2023 was skeptical and slow, still reeling from the post-COVID swing. But I didn't want that factor to define us, so I started calling it FUNdraising. I wrote the word—yes, all caps—on every pitch deck, spreadsheet, and doc we shared. It was a small shift in language that helped reframe the task. FUNdraising wasn't about chasing checks; it was about finding people who believed in what we were building. And our first benchmark was to secure a lead investor who validated us and helped set the terms so we could close the round.

Our friend Mike Posner made a few introductions, and one of them led us to that lead investor, who happened to be his cousin. His firm didn't just write a half-a-million-dollar check—they understood us. They saw the vision, the culture, the kingdom we were building, and wanted to help strengthen it. We gave them a seat on the board and welcomed them in as partners in our mission.

During the rest of the summer and early fall, we settled into a rhythm of Ironman training, pitch meetings, follow-ups, investor calls, and late-night deck edits. We knocked on every door in our network and beyond, taking well over a hundred calls. It was exhausting. Some days felt like tunneling through soil blindfolded, relying only on faith and instinct.

But we got there. We closed the round at $1.3 million raised.

For the first time, we had enough capital to ramp up production, fulfill orders without weeks of backlogs, invest in research and development, and keep the marketing engine running.

Through it all, the image of that painted tree stayed with me. There on my phone screen, still reaching out with its branches of silent wisdom and whispering what I most needed to hear. *Keep going. This is the growth you asked for.*

CHAPTER 20

Built For Winter

The momentum from fundraising carried us into late fall like a rising tide that refused to crest, pulling us straight to the starting line of the Ironman in November. The celebration of crossing that finish line was only made sweeter by the joy of closing out that month at over $2 million in sales. We were riding high.

That euphoric full-circle moment was worth every painful step I'd taken to find my edge, both personally and professionally. And to celebrate it with the team of trusted colleagues who had enthusiastically gone *all in* on this dream of building something meaningful together will forever remain one of the most cherished highlights of my life.

When we closed the books on 2023, the numbers confirmed that we hadn't just hit our goal, we had more than doubled it. Revenue had exceeded $12 million. More than 2,000 lives changed through cold exposure, using a product we had brought into the world. It was staggering, beautiful, and completely humbling.

As the year drew to a close, Rob and I began preparing for another Team Development Day. We could feel the temptation to chase the next big number, to stretch for $20 million, but something inside us resisted.

The landscape of our industry was clearly shifting. The cold tub market was heating up fast, and we were no longer alone. Knockoffs and imitators were popping up like weeds after rain; everyone and their mother suddenly seemed to be selling cold tubs. There were whispers of big players eyeing the space. What we had built was being noticed. And somewhere just beyond the horizon, we could feel a gathering pressure. Winter was coming.

While the world prepared to ring in the new year with champagne and countdowns, Rob and I stayed late at the office. The clock edged past eight, then nine. Outside, the sky held the quiet electricity of New Year's Eve. Inside, we sat shoulder to shoulder at the conference table, poring over budget drafts, fine-tuning forecasts, and realigning our vision to send to our Board of Directors. We felt like we were boarding a ship in the dark, navigating by instinct and the faint starlight of what we'd learned the prior year. We settled on a new target: $15 million in revenue. Still ambitious, but grounded and achievable.

One of our boldest moves in the year ahead—backed fully by our lead investor—was launching a mobile application. I had long dreamed of it, ever since guiding friends through breathwork and plunges on my back deck. The vision was to create a digital companion to the ritual. Like Calm or Headspace, but specifically designed for cold immersion, breathwork, and heat therapy. A space where anyone, anywhere, could press play and receive guidance, track their progress, and deepen their practice. Because we weren't just selling tubs. We were building habits, cultivating community, and creating an ecosystem.

Stepping into the frost-lined dawn of 2024, we set our sights on three clear objectives. First, to sell three thousand tubs, generating $15 million in revenue. Second, to launch the Edge App, and third, to part ways with our original manufacturer and begin production on Gen 2: a refined version of the Edge Tub, born from every lesson we had paid for in full.

One afternoon, during an Executive Team meeting, while discussing the product quality issues, the stale office air seemed to echo our frustration. The last sip of Rob's afternoon pot of coffee had gone cold at the bottom of my mug. I rubbed my temples, staring again at the numbers on the screen.

"This partnership is broken," I muttered, more to myself than to the room.

TJ didn't look up. "They're robbing us blind," he said, deadpan, sliding another report across the table. "I've never worked with a factory this disrespectful. Ever."

Rob leaned in, brow furrowed. "Even after millions in orders, they're still refusing to give us a price break. And they're not reimbursing us for what we are spending to fix their issues."

"It's not just the money," I said, scrolling through a string of emails. "They lie. They gaslight. Every time we report failures, they act like we're making it up."

The room fell quiet. We had started with these partners in good faith—grateful just to have found anyone who could manufacture at scale. And yes, they helped us get to market. But now, the underbelly of that partnership had fully surfaced.

"They're selling our chiller to other brands," Rob said quietly, staring at the floor. "Our own manufacturer is our competitor."

"Every improvement we've made over the past two years," TJ added, "has been a free upgrade for the knockoffs. We've been funding their R&D."

We'd had first-mover advantage, yes—but also the first-mover burden. Every bug, every pissed-off customer with a unit that couldn't hold temperature, was ours to handle. Since we didn't have exclusivity or a patent, each problem we solved made the product better, not just for us, but for our competitors who manufactured with our supplier.

"What matters now," I said slowly, "is that we take care of our customers, the people who believe in us. If we have to eat the cost, so be it. We'll hire the support and replace the units. We're not going to leave anyone hanging. We do business the right way."

Rob nodded. "That's it. That's the only thing that matters. Our brand is built on trust, and trust is everything."

February marked a different kind of turning point. It was the first month we ever missed our sales targets—and the first month we lost money. The pressure was mounting, quietly but unmistakably. Our biggest competitor had just announced a new product nearly identical to ours, threatening the one thing we thought made us unique. At the same time, the cost of acquiring customers was rising like a thick, slow fog seeping through the cracks of what we'd built. With lingering product issues and growing support costs, the profitable engine we'd crafted was starting to sputter.

Rob and I spent more nights than we could count holed up in the conference room, whiteboards filled, takeout boxes stacked, updating spreadsheets until the rows blurred together. Adjusting forecasts, demand plans, and scenario models felt like trying to catch a moving train while we were already sprinting as fast as we could go.

We told ourselves spring would bring a thaw—longer days, warmer weather, more orders. Until then, we were trying to sell cold tubs to a country still buried in snow. Like selling ice to Eskimos. I couldn't decide whether our predicament was a hurdle we could eventually clear or a strangely poetic scenario.

But even in the thick of those obstacles, there were bright spots that carried us forward. Sam, Nikita and I hosted our first ever Edge Winter Retreat in Jackson Hole Wyoming, delivering a deep transformation to our community who came. Chad and I flew to Orlando for the NFL Trainers' Conference. Our booth was buzzing, and we closed big deals worth dozens of tubs. Even more importantly, we started a conversation with the Los Angeles Rams' performance staff that turned into something bigger. Not just a sale, but a brand partnership. We'd become the official cold tub provider for the LA Rams.

The morning I flew home from Orlando from the NFL conference, I joined a Zoom call with our European app team at 5:00 a.m. Eastern Time from a quiet airport corner, walking through UX updates. I worked straight through the cross-country flight, took an Uber directly to the office, and worked until a 7:00 p.m. meeting with Rob. We left after 9:00 that evening. A 19-hour workday, and I was still lit up. That rhythm didn't drain me; it reminded me of those training camp days in San Francisco with Ricky and early mornings in the Santa Monica apartment with the boys.

The Edge App launched with a splash and started gaining traction early, but we quickly realized we'd just launched a whole new company inside the company. It needed attention, real time, and resources that we were already spreading thin. We were now juggling two businesses and barely keeping up with either.

By May, the market had exploded. Cold tub startups were popping up weekly, and most faded just as fast. They hadn't yet learned what we already had: selling a tub is easy, standing behind it is the hard part. Some copied our site word for word—literally. One even forgot to swap out our name. "Edge" was still sitting on their homepage.

Thankfully, I had a breadcrumb already on the calendar—a coaching call with my mindset coach and mentor, Giorgio.

I decided to take the call out of the office. I walked across the train tracks and followed the path to the bluff above the water, where the sun was folding into the horizon in golds and violets, and the wind off the cliffs brushed against my skin. I sat for a moment, letting the heaviness rise. I felt distant from the parts of this journey that once lit me up—the spark from

Iceland, the joy of our early wins. This tangled mess of logistics and supply chain wasn't the dream. Sales were slipping, stress was high, and when Giorgio picked up, I didn't hold back. I let it spill out—the fatigue, the fear, the weight of wondering if we were losing our way.

He listened quietly, then said just one thing. "Don't get lost in the sauce. You're struggling because you're trying to compete on product. But you're not just selling a tub, mate. You're selling transformation."

I stopped walking. The breeze touched my face as his words sank into me like roots. He was right. The tub had always been a portal—not to the cold, but to connection with your mind and body.

When I returned to the office, dusk had settled. Everyone was gone, and the quiet felt holy. I went straight to the sauna to sit in this new perspective. I thought about how the cold had healed me. Not just my body, but my soul. I thought about the people—our team, our customers. The ones who had found their edge and come back changed. I thought about the email we got from the random customer who was a veteran suffering from PTSD and wrote to us to tell us that getting into our cold tub was the first time he felt relief from his symptoms, that this experience had literally saved his life. And I realized, once again, this business wasn't about me or the tubs. It never had been.

I stepped out of the sauna with sweat still dripping and the towel slung around my waist, and made my way to my standing desk. Harry Reid's usual shirt-and-shoes policy was, gratefully, suspended at this hour. The note taped to my monitor—*They're waiting for you*—met my eyes like it was brand new. I opened a blank doc. What came wasn't a sales plan or roadmap. It was a reframe. A script for a video I knew we needed to create to position ourselves differently and plant our flag in the sand. It felt less like a pivot and more like a homecoming.

I wrote:

> We live in a world where we've never been more sick, isolated and disconnected. That's why we set out to create an ecosystem at Edge Theory Labs where a new level of health is unlocked, deep connections are built, and lasting transformation is the norm—because our job doesn't stop when we ship your product. That's where it begins.
>
> We're focused on three key pillars to bring this to life: product, education, and community.
>
> Firstly, we support you with the innovative tools for your transformation. We created the highest quality and most practical cold tub at the most affordable price, and now with our Edge App, we're set on making these practices more accessible than ever before. And beyond a reliable product, our team is here to support you every step of the way.
>
> Secondly, we want to help you understand the science and benefits of these practices—demystifying the Wild West and pop culture trends of ice baths, of breath work, and heat therapy. We provide digestible educational content and guided protocols on our Edge App, all backed by our esteemed Scientific Advisory Board and leading team of Edge Coaches.
>
> And last, but certainly not least: community—the glue that ties everything together. As we like to say at Edge: friend power is stronger than willpower.
>
> The Legends community is vibrant, filled with thousands of like-minded high performers from all around the world, pushing their perceived limitations every single day. Whether it's meeting new friends at our events in person, tuning into virtual events on the Edge App, or joining a life-changing retreat—become a part of a community that lifts you up.
>
> These core pillars of innovative product, science-backed education, and like-minded community create the perfect

> *ecosystem for sustainable transformation. This is what we're here to do. We've got your back with unwavering support every step of the way.*
>
> *You've got this. And we've got you. Let's Go All In.*

Once again, taking responsibility and facing the challenge head-on helped us rebuild momentum. We launched a video that struck a chord, and rewrote the website copy to reflect what we were really about. Chad started weaving that same language into sales calls, and we saw an increase in conversion rate. People understood us—because we finally understood ourselves.

The days that followed felt lighter. We'd been reminded of a hard but useful truth about winter: you either freeze or you adapt. It reveals where things aren't strong enough yet. The frustration of rising competition had turned into clarity. It pushed us to go deeper, to stand more firmly in who we really were, which turned out to be a gift. The breadcrumb made of coal had, in fact, become the diamond it was always meant to be.

There will always be winters. But spring always rises from the snow, carrying its quiet promise.

And we believed our brightest days were still ahead.

CHAPTER 21

Setting the Temperature

THAT SPRING, WE WATCHED THE DASHBOARDS with quiet hope and clenched jaws, waiting for the seasonal lift we'd come to rely on. But it never came. Sales held flat, stubborn and unmoved. Month over month, we were bleeding cash hand over fist. Warranty claims and repair requests rolled in like a flood breaching our sandbags. We'd tried everything to hold off the inevitable, but the wave had finally arrived.

Numbers don't lie, and ours revealed the brutal reality. It was time to make cuts—not just to snacks or software subscriptions, but to paychecks. Our teammates. Rob and I circled the decision for weeks, hoping a miracle would come through. But eventually, the math forced our hand.

"Better to do this now than risk the whole thing later," he said one evening, quietly, from across the table. We both sat in the silence that followed. This wasn't the kind of weariness that sleep could fix.

These were our friends. The ones who helped build this dream with us. That week, we let go of three full-time team members and a few contractors. There was no easy way to do it, only the hope we could do it with integrity. We leaned into those conversations with honesty, presence, and a deep desire to honor the trust they had given us. There were tears, long pauses, but also grace. A mutual understanding of the reality we were facing. And respect I'll never forget.

That day required something of me I'd been training for quietly over the years—the ability to sit in hard things without flinching. To hold tension, breathe through discomfort, and still show up authentically. To carry the weight of someone else's new uncertainty, and still focus on the work in front of me. It was a test of presence. And something told me there would be more tests ahead.

After those brutal conversations, the office was quiet. Rob and I sat in the somber stillness of what came next. We had built a team and infrastructure designed to support a $15-$20 million business. Now we were forced to align with a reality that was 50 percent of our expectations. We had to rework the plan with leaner parts and lighter fuel.

Amid the haze of early summer, with sales stalled, morale bruised, and layoffs still fresh, a glimmer of hope appeared: Syochi. From our first conversation with this new chiller manufacturer, it was clear the dynamic would be different. Their team was responsive, reliable, and aligned in values. With better communication, real accountability, and even a 30 percent cost savings per unit, Syochi appeared not just as a supplier but a partner that could help turn things around. But we would need to bring our new product to market fast to make it work.

Hope returned, not in some big, dramatic way, but gently, like the first breeze after a long, hot season. The new framework of our Edge Theory Labs brand focused on transformation. I went back to the basics and focused on what would bring me energy and deliver transformation right in front of me.

I put out a simple invite for a free Sunday morning breathwork session. That first week, fifteen people showed up in the back parking lot of our office. We laid out yoga mats under the open sky, and it felt so good to be of service. So I did it again. And again. More people came each time. We called it Sunrise Social Club.

Then I teamed up with my yoga-teacher friend, who brought her community. The following weekend, I looked up from my yoga mat to see the entire lot full—nearly a hundred people lying on mats, hands over hearts, tears sliding down cheeks. We needed to find another space for this party.

The next breadcrumb was waiting for me that next week. I received a message out of the blue from a girl I hadn't spoken to since high school. She worked in commercial real estate and, unbeknownst to me, had been following our adventures.

"I think you should see something," she wrote. Curious, I agreed to meet.

She showed me a retail space that was connected to my apartment building, of all places, and offered us a sweetheart of a deal to take over a vacant storefront where we could offer a sauna, breathwork, and cold plunge studio. Though it was tempting, the timing wasn't right. As we wrapped up our meeting, though, I glanced across the promenade toward the lawn that extended wide and open, framed by palm trees and perfect morning light.

"What about that spot?" I asked. "Could we host something there?"

She paused, looked across the green space, and nodded. "Yeah. I don't see why not!"

When we moved Sunrise Social Club to the lawn, it caught fire. Before we knew it, two hundred people were showing up. Every other Sunday, we hauled tubs, ice, our Ledgends merch line, towels, and signage. Cat ran point on orchestrating every detail. My younger sister Rachel helped run the check-in table and rallied people to show up. I stood barefoot in the grass, mic'd up to a sound system, and guided hundreds through breath and presence. I watched strangers connect and hearts soften. I saw people remember who they are. I was both exhausted and fully alive in the same breath. And I kept coming back to the same quiet truth: every time I return to *the why*, the path forward reveals itself again.

It became clear. This isn't just a business. This is what I'm here to do.

That summer, I flew to Europe for a friend's wedding. The trip was supposed to be a pause so I could catch my breath from a year that had become increasingly difficult to navigate. After the celebration, I boarded a train north, leaving Italy behind and heading into the Alps toward Germany, where I planned to visit another friend.

The train wound through pine-covered hills and past serene lakes, scenery that usually brings me peace. But, just as I started to settle into a daydream, entranced by the view outside the train's window, my phone buzzed. It was Rob.

I answered with a half-smile. "Hey, brother."

His voice had an edge. "We need to talk, dude. Sales aren't where they need to be. And we just got hit with a few big bills. Our cash position is bad."

I shifted in my seat, earbuds in, glancing down at the ground. "How bad?"

"We're not going to make payroll next month unless we make more cuts. And we've already trimmed the fat. Now it's going to be muscle."

I sighed, watching the trees blur past. "Copy that. We'll do what we have to do."

"We've got to stop all non-essential spending," he said. "Stretch vendor payments. And...we'll need to pull more from the line of credit."

That last one hit hard. We'd already dipped into the credit line once. Pulling from it again meant stacking interest and pushing the problem down the road in hopes that the road didn't lead us off a cliff.

There was a long pause.

"Okay," I said. "We'll figure it out. We always do."

We hung up just as the train entered a tunnel, and the cabin dimmed. I stared at my reflection in the glass, the darkness outside mirroring how I felt inside. There was no magic fix here, just decisions to make and actions to take. So much felt out of my control.

In Munich, a teacher was waiting for me with the next breadcrumb. John, an old friend and one of our earliest investors in Edge, opened the door of his apartment to greet me.

He stood six-foot-four with an athletic build, his shaggy brown hair curling at the ends, his eyes bright and focused. I noticed immediately that he looked clear-headed, grounded, not to mention ridiculously fit. His calm presence caught me off guard because I knew what he was carrying. His company was also unraveling, at a scale far larger than ours. Hundreds of employees, global offices, revenue in the hundreds of millions, yet here he was barefoot in his kitchen, steaming vegetables, asking how *I* was doing.

We spent a few days together that came at just the right time. We took walks by the river, with his dog, Mia, prancing beside us, and savored three-hour meals where he greeted every server by name and exchanged inside jokes with them. Sun-soaked afternoons stretched out on the grass, we felt like two kids at summer camp. One evening, we sat out on his balcony while the Munich skyline softened in the distance, music drifted outside from his record player. I told him everything. The cash flow crunch, the layoffs, the pressure to keep going when so much felt uncertain. He just listened, patiently and steadily, then leaned forward and said something that would stay with me.

"You've got to control the controllables," he said. "Grab the reins and do what needs to be done." Then he added, "Be the thermostat, not the thermometer."

I looked over, not quite getting it at first. He smiled. "You set the temperature," he said. "You decide the tone. Don't just react to the room. Change it."

The simplicity of it hit me. He wasn't speaking from theory. He was living it. His discipline in the middle of a collapse was intentional. He reminded me that, no matter what's happening externally, you can regulate your own internal climate and choose calm over panic, focus over frenzy, and breath over noise. That's what leadership really is. It's learning to hold your own center so you can bring warmth, clarity, and steadiness to any room, even when everything around you seems to be spinning on ice—especially then.

I flew back to San Diego with his words still echoing in my mind. Nothing about our situation had changed. The numbers were still tight, the choices still hard, but something in me felt steadier. I committed to focusing only on what was mine to carry and let go of the rest. Control the controllables and let the Universe handle the heavy lifting, which it was so good at. After all, the sun continued to rise without needing any of my help.

My job was simple. *Set the temperature.*

CHAPTER 22

Man in the Arena

I TEXT ROB THE MOMENT MY PLANE lands back in San Diego. It's Monday evening, and I'm home from Europe with a fire in my chest, ready to charge back into the storm. His reply comes fast: "Daughter was born today!"

A flash of light in the fog. My heart lifts, and I drive straight from the airport to his house, suitcase still in the trunk.

The house is hushed when I arrive. Rob greets me at the door with tired eyes and a soft smile. He leads me to the nursery, where his wife is holding their newborn baby, and I meet his daughter for the first time. She is barely the size of a football, swaddled in a blush-pink blanket, her face impossibly serene. We sit quietly in his living room, surrounded by baby bottles and blankets, soaked in the sweetness that follows birth.

Rob looks over, eyes damp. "She's everything," he says.

Later that night, I collapsed into a hug with the girl I had started dating right in the middle of those difficult months. Though we were casually dating, she felt like solid ground. The one constant that felt consistent and reliable.

By sunrise Tuesday, I'm at the office, jet-lagged but alive. The glow of Slack messages, scribbles on whiteboards, and the quiet diligence of the early hours charge me up. But the picture

Rob painted while I was away hadn't captured the full scope of what we were facing. The numbers were worse than I expected.

That week, our refunds had outpaced sales. Our inventory was draining faster than forecasted, and the cash flow document resembled a bloodbath. Payroll is due in two weeks, and we don't have the money. Our line of credit is now maxed out.

For hours, I wrestle with how to shield Rob. He deserves to stay in that newborn bubble just a little longer. But this can't wait.

"Rob," I text, "I'm really sorry to do this, but we need to talk."

He tells me to come over. We sit in lawn chairs in his backyard, the sun shining bright, birds chirping like nothing's wrong. His daughter sleeps inside, and his wife is resting. But out here, it's war.

"Yeah, like I said while you were in Europe, we're going to have to make some deep cuts," he says, shaking his head, clearly frustrated that I came over just to tell him what he already knew.

"No, Rob, you don't understand, this isn't a next month problem. We're going to miss *this* payroll. Sales over the last two weeks have come in at half of what we expected."

He leans back, eyes skyward, fixed on the treetops. His silence says everything. His countenance reveals the stress of a man now responsible for a newborn and a collapsing business.

"Shit," he mutters.

Two days later, Rob walks into the office. He's not supposed to be here. The team sees him and knows something's wrong. We gather everyone and speak plainly, from the heart. We let go of two more team members. They were necessary cuts, but we know that still may not be enough.

I leave the office after thirteen hours of meetings that day and dial Rob from my car, voice thin, body empty.

"Well," I joke, "at least the day's over. Can't get worse, right?"

I get home, drop my keys, and my phone buzzes. A message from the girl I'm dating. "Hey, we need to talk. Can you come over?"

"Tonight's not great," I text back. "Still have a few hours of work ahead. Can we talk tomorrow?"

She replies instantly. "Fine. I'll come to you."

Minutes later, she's at the door, her face is somber.

"I can't do this anymore."

And with that, another pillar falls. She leaves, and I don't stop her. I just sit there, staring blankly into the stillness, the only thing to comfort me is the steady whir of my Edge Tub on the balcony. The weight of everything presses in like a hurricane gathering at nightfall.

There's another buzz on my phone. This one reveals a quote from Teddy Roosevelt that Rob texted me.

> *"It is not the critic who counts; not the man who points out how the strong man stumbles, or where the doer of deeds could have done them better. The credit belongs to the man who is actually in the arena, whose face is marred by dust and sweat and blood; who strives valiantly; who errs, who comes short again and again, because there is no effort without error and shortcoming; but who does actually strive to do the deeds; who knows the great enthusiasms, the great devotions; who spends himself in a worthy cause; who at the best knows in the end the triumph of high achievement, and who at the worst, if he fails, at least fails while daring greatly, so that his place shall never be with those cold and timid souls who neither know victory nor defeat."*

He didn't need to say anything else. We were in the arena. And what a privilege that was.

With Rob on paternity leave, I stepped fully into War Time CEO mode. One day, I was juggling the chaos, the next I was cutting through it. Leadership meant calling hard shots, and this was no time to flinch. I tightened the reins and pulled our core team into the center of the storm with me.

We gathered in the conference room. Once a buzzing hub, it now feels hollow with our team dwindling. The windows were cracked to let in the San Diego breeze, but the air felt dense with unspoken tension. I stood at the head of the table, scanning the faces I respected, trusted, and cared for. These weren't just coworkers. They were friends who had poured themselves into this dream alongside us.

"I need to be honest with you," I said. "We're not just in a tough spot; it's critical."

I laid it all out with zero fluff. We were officially in save-the-company mode. Radical transparency became our north star. There was no sugarcoating. Rob and I shared everything—numbers, risks, worst-case scenarios. And oddly, the honesty brought us all closer. It made us stronger and more aligned. The team showed up. The culture we'd built was being tested, and our key players rose to the occasion.

Inside, I felt tangled by a thousand vines. I kept picturing a forest. I saw myself hacking through brush with no trail in sight, just praying for one clearing. One patch of ground that beckons: *this way.* In the quiet moments, when no one was around, I'd whisper the same question to myself over and over: *How nobly can you face this? How nobly can you endure?* Nobility became my compass. This wasn't about pretending things were fine. It was about holding the line with integrity, even when I felt like everything was unraveling.

Some days, I felt like a gladiator. Standing tall. "Bring it on," I'd mutter under my breath, chest out.

Other days, I was wrecked. Staring through bloodshot eyes at spreadsheets long past midnight, angry and drained, muttering, "Fuck this."

Then there were the shadowy days, the ones where grief crept in—the inconsolable ache of feeling this dream we had poured everything into slip through our fingers.

We were deep in the trenches. Every hour accounted for, every dollar tracked, and every conversation heavy. There were no fantasies of $50 million years ahead or glossy headlines proclaiming our success; just the next move, and then the next.

We did have one shot left. A rare, narrow opening presented itself in the fall of that year. Months earlier, a producer from a famous business television show—the same one I'd grown up watching from my parents' couch—had reached out. He'd seen our story, liked the product, and invited us to audition. At the time, we were flattered and thought it might be fun. We took the call, went through the motions, and we were assigned a film date. But now, the opportunity took on a different weight. This wasn't about exposure, ego, or vanity metrics; it was about survival. And an investment from this show could buy us time to right the ship.

After a tense board call, we made the decision. We were going all in. The show became our moonshot, our Hail Mary. If we walked away with an investment, we'd have the capital to carry us through the winter, ride out the storm, and get our Gen 2 tub to market. With a leaner team and a new manufacturer in place, maybe—just maybe—we could rebuild. And if we couldn't, then we would pivot our plan to explore a merger or acquisition with a company that might value our community and marketing engine. That certainly wasn't the dream, but it felt like the only option.

In the days leading up to filming, the energy around the team became tighter, stronger, and more electric. This was happening. We were about to pitch Edge Theory Labs to the most well-known investors in the world, for a national television audience, on the very stage that had raised our entrepreneurial ambitions as teenagers. I kept thinking about the scrappy kids we used to be—Rob and me in that hotel room, stashing the Laser Lynx blueprints into the safe, Chad and I dreaming in the basement of our Fraternity house, and meeting Cat while we were still figuring out life on the west coast. I could almost see those younger versions of us fistpumping in the wings, cheering us on from across time.

One afternoon, as we wrapped a final prep session, I paused and looked around the room.

"I just want to say," I said, locking in on every set of eyes around the table, "I love you. Every one of you." There were a few chuckles and a few choked-up nods.

By now, Chad had become a lifeline. Our meetings weren't just about sales strategy; they were reminders of everything we were working towards. He reminded me of the stats. LeBron James missed 28 game-winning shots. Michael Jordan missed even more. But they kept showing up. Kept asking for the ball. Because success isn't built on avoiding misses, it's built on taking the shot. It's forged by how you show up when the heat is on, when the crowd goes silent, when the ending hasn't yet been written.

We knew it in our bones: this was our moment. Our chance to save the company.

The studio was ice-cold, even under the hot lights. Cameras positioned like sentinels. Producers whispered behind the Steadicam. Rob stood beside me. We bumped fists. My heart pounded, but my mind was still. We were ready. We had memorized over eighty flashcards—every stat, every response, every angle covered. It was game time.

A producer stepped in front of us, arm raised like a conductor. "Five. Four." Then the silent count—three, two, one. And a point.

The double doors flew open.

We walked forward, each step silent and steady. The camera operator backed down the hallway in front of us, tracking our movement like a mirror. Another set of doors opened. And there it was—the iconic set I'd seen so many times through a television screen. Glossy floors. Harsh lights. And at the far end, the five investors, seated in full suits and business attire in an unmoving arc of chairs.

For a moment, it felt like a dream. Like we had projected this from our imaginations onto a real stage, but this was no dream. Every breath, every light, every heartbeat in that room was real.

So we stepped forward, into the arena.

CHAPTER 23

This Is The Fun, You See

"I'M SORRY, BUT I'M OUT," THE last investor says. Her tone is firm but kind, the way a teacher might let a student down gently.

"Thanks so much for coming," she adds, offering a warm smile. "You should be really proud of what you've built. Even though I'm not investing, I'll definitely be a customer. Best of luck moving forward."

And just like that, it's over. The opportunity vanishes before we can catch our breath. We turn and walk off the stage. The lights behind us dim slightly. The door closes behind us, and the weight of disappointment begins to settle into my body. It's a slow, quiet sinking, like silt drifting to the bottom of a lake after a storm.

We'd been in there for nearly thirty minutes. Thirty minutes of pitching, redirecting, negotiating, and defending. Thirty minutes of five brilliant minds coming at us from every angle. Their voices overlapped, questions stacked in unpredictable rhythms, each new question arriving before the last could be answered. What you don't see in the clean, edited-for-TV segment is how impossible it is to steer the conversation when five people are talking over each other, each one racing to get their question in first. It was a test of composure with barely any space to breathe.

They liked us, our mission, and our numbers. But they didn't like where we were trending with flat growth, a tight cash runway, and the loss of profitability. And, honestly, we didn't like it either.

We were ushered off-set to a side stage draped in heavy black curtains for a quick follow-up interview. The lights were softer there, but still glared with a certain intensity, like lightning from a storm that hadn't fully passed.

After the interview wrapped, Rob and I gave each other a long, silent hug. There wasn't much left to say. We had left everything on that stage—emptied the tank, walked into the arena, and done our best. We didn't get the outcome we had hoped for, but there was quiet satisfaction in how we showed up. In how we stood firm under pressure, took the hits, and didn't flinch.

A stagehand escorted us back toward the green room while I sent up a silent prayer. Or, more accurately, a whispered request to the Universe. *Please—give me another sign. Show me we're still on the right path. That even in the wake of this disappointment, we're exactly where we need to be.*

When I turned the corner, I noticed one of the camera operators—the same guy who'd filmed our post-show interview—was wearing a faded Cleveland Indians hat, worn down at the seams from years of wear and tear.

"Nice hat," I said, casually.

"Thanks, man," he replied with a grin. "You from Cleveland?"

"Yeah," I nodded. "Rob and I both lived there when we were kids. Our dads grew up there."

He laughed. "Small world! Cleveland people always find each other."

"Yeah, we really do," I said, a smile creeping in. "What part are you from?"

"Lakewood," he said.

I stopped mid-step. Rob turned around, too.

"No way," I said. "That's where our dads grew up. They both went to Lakewood High."

His face changed instantly. "I went to Lakewood High," he said, slower now.

I glanced at Rob, a bolt of curiosity passing between us. The man looked about our dads' age. I decided to take the long shot.

"Did you ever know a Bill or Jeff Church?"

His mouth fell slightly open. For a second, he didn't say a word. He just stood there, motionless.

"Bill and Jeff were my neighbors," he said at last, his voice a little stunned. "I grew up playing football in the street with them. I was a few years younger, but they always included me. We lived right there on Clifton Road."

We stood in silence, all three of us. Smiling with that unmistakable feeling that none of this was random. It was a message, delivered right on time, written in divine handwriting. A soft ray of light tucked into the aftermath of a hard moment. Another cosmic breadcrumb reminded us we were still on the path.

When I stepped back into the green room, I carried a slight smile on my face and a strange sense of peace in my chest. That conversation was my sign. I was reminded, even in the face of disappointment, that even when our path isn't clear or easy, we are still on it—still being guided, still in the game.

September turned to October. The nights cooled, the days shortened, and we found ourselves racing against a clock we could not ignore. The show hadn't given us the lifeline we hoped for, so now we pivoted into full merger mode—searching for rafts in waters that were growing colder by the day.

Each promising call with an industry founder brought a flicker of hope that dimmed just as quickly as it arrived. One potential partner, a cold tub company out of Australia, seemed aligned. But our timelines didn't match up, so that door closed. We felt a glimmer of hope just long enough to get excited before another letdown.

Along came three more conversations, then a fourth. Each started strong before dissolving into silence. Every *no* landed with a heartbreaking thud.

We kept returning to the whiteboard, asking the same question: *What now?*

Soon, Rob and I were forced to face the question we swore we'd never ask. The one you lock away in the attic of your mind and hope never creeps down the stairs.

What if we have to shut it down?

We didn't say it out loud at first; we just felt it moving through the room between us like a shadow, heavy and uninvited.

During that season, something small but significant began to shift inside me. There was a subtle rearranging in my chest, like the furniture of my faith was being moved in the dark. For years, I'd spoken to the Universe—that great current of synchronicity I believed in, the unseen force behind cosmic breadcrumbs and perfect timing. It had always felt expansive and mysterious in a way that left room for wonder.

But when the nights grew longer and the pressure around us tightened like a slow-closing fist, "Universe" began to feel too distant, too impersonal, like calling out into a canyon and hearing only your own echo.

What I needed wasn't a vague force or poetic abstraction. I needed a real presence. I needed a hand to hold in the dark. I needed to speak to something—or someone—that could listen. And answer.

So I started to pray. Not to the Universe, but to God. The Creator of the Universe. The artist behind the architecture. The one who not only knows the shape of the stars but also the weight in my chest. The one who doesn't just move mountains, but sits with me when I can't climb them. I felt how the shift in the name shifted my relationship with the divine, almost like the quiet milestone of graduating from calling Mommy "Mom".

The hardest part during that time wasn't the fear; it was the split energy. One foot in the arena, still fighting for the miracle of a merger or acquisition, and the other hovering at the edge of the end, not knowing what was going to happen. We lived in the daily dichotomy between fighting for survival to keep the company afloat and simultaneously considering a plan to close up shop to avoid burning our employees by missing payroll or showing up at our office one day to find the doors locked. No business book I'd read ever taught me how to navigate this.

Right on time, Chad's text lit up my phone. A quote from Alan Watts:

"Don't be afraid. You're going to make it, but it's always going to feel as if you're not. That's the fun, you see!"

What if this *is* the fun of it? Maybe the not-knowing isn't punishment. Maybe it's the gift. Because if we knew how every chapter ends, we'd lose the thrill of turning the page. We play the game because we *don't* know the outcome. The uncertainty, the ache, the edge of it all—that's the moment when life grins and dares you to keep playing. It's the part of the movie where the music swells and the audience leans forward, popcorn in hand, whispering, *"What's he going to do next?"* Maybe that's what makes it worth watching and worth living. The suspense means the story's still unfolding.

In this torrid purgatory, which stretched for weeks, my most intimate prayer became: *God, please lead me where you need me most. I'll follow. Just show me the way.*

And strangely, this new perspective softened me. The surrender wasn't dramatic or tear-streaked—it was quiet, like arriving at my gate at the airport and setting down my backpack to only then realize how heavy it was. And in that stillness, I felt something return. A familiar presence and unmistakably clear whisper, like a breeze moving through a curtain, came to me: *I'm still here. How much do you trust me?*

And for the first time in weeks, I decided to trust it fully. Tension was stretching us thin, but we kept walking. And for the moment, that was enough.

Reality hit hard the next morning. It was Monday, and Rob and I met for our usual one-on-one walk. That rhythm had been sacred over the years, a standing tradition to step outside the building and process whatever storm we were navigating. Only this time, the walk stretched longer than usual. We kept circling the industrial blocks of Carlsbad's coastal business park, the sun high overhead, our bodies wound tight with tension. Neither of us had much left to hide.

"Where are you at with it all, Rob?" I asked as we rounded another corner.

He didn't answer right away. His face was blank, but not absent—just worn down by exhaustion. Finally, with a tired exhale, he said, "I'm exhausted, man. I've been burnt out since the summer. And now, with my daughter here…it's hitting different. I'm at a real breaking point."

"I hear you," I said quietly. "I'm not far behind, man."

We walked in silence, the gravel crunching beneath our shoes. The world felt oddly hushed.

"I just don't see a way through this," Rob finally said. "We've cut everything we can cut. There's nothing left. And now we're heading into winter—our slowest season—with zero marketing budget and more competition than ever."

I nodded, the words landing in my chest like stones. "It feels like we're flooring the gas pedal toward a cliff," I said. "And I'm afraid we're going to go down in flames."

There was only one thing left to do. We needed to bring it to the board, lay it all out, and see what they had to say.

That night, we got to work. We stayed late, pulled up every document, combed through financials, built out models, and mapped every possible scenario. None of them looked good. Each path led to a brick wall. Some options were more painful than others—but all of them felt like defeat.

When we sat down with the board later that week, we presented the numbers, timelines, and constraints we were facing. The board listened closely, asked their questions, and took their time. Eventually, they came to the same conclusion we had.

The most responsible course of action would be an orderly wind-down. Liquidate our assets while we still have the chance to do it right and avoid a catastrophe wherever possible.

The vote was unanimous. And just like that, the last chapter was being written.

After the meeting, Rob and I sat in silence. There was grief and fear. Of course, there was. We had given it everything we had. But underneath the ache, a strange peace began to surface. The weight of uncertainty had lifted. Replaced by something heavier, maybe, but at least it had a name.

No more split energy. No more wondering if we'd pull it off or fall flat. We had our answer.

Questions rushed in faster than we could answer them.

How would we tell the team?

What would we say to the people who had ridden through the storm with us?

What about our inventory? Our customers? The vendors still waiting on payment? The back taxes? The office lease that Rob and I were personally liable for? The debt we owed our secured creditor?

What would we tell our investors? Our friends, family, professional athletes who had gone out on a limb? The people who believed and backed us with their money?

How do we tell them we'd lost it?

How do we say, *"We did everything we could, but it wasn't enough"*?

There were no clean answers. No easy conversations. Just the next hard step.

That evening after the board call, I had to compartmentalize everything. The decision to shut down was still ringing in my chest like an aftershock, but I'd made plans to attend a San Diego Padres playoff baseball game with a friend and his wife. A high school friend, who was also an investor, played for the rival Dodgers and was in town for a heated matchup. I was in no mood to go, but I showed up anyway, dazed and heavy, carrying the news of the day like a knot in my gut.

On the drive to the stadium, I whispered a prayer. I didn't even think about it. I just said it, like an instinct.

God, I need to know you're still with me. Just send a sign. On this day, of all days, I need to feel you near.

We found our seats, which were high up and tucked beneath an overhang. During the first inning, my friend's wife said with a smile, "Maybe we'll catch a foul ball."

"Impossible," my friend replied, barely glancing up. "Not from here."

And then, it happened.

In a scene stranger than fiction, after the very next pitch, a ball cracked off the bat and began to rise. Unnaturally high. It kept climbing toward the overhang, higher than it had any right to, defying the angles. People in our section stood up, craning their necks in disbelief.

The ball soared past the net, threading through the only open pocket in the structure above our heads. Without flinching or moving an inch, my friend raised his arm, and the ball landed squarely in his right hand like it had been thrown directly to him by something unseen.

We all froze. Then burst out laughing, shaking our heads in utter amazement.

Once we stopped laughing and sat down, I looked down at my hands, folded in my lap, and couldn't help but smile. My friend handed me the ball.

God wasn't just present in the big miracles or the loud salvations. He was in the small, playful moments, too. The kind of wink that reminds you to keep looking up. That you're still being led. Still on the path—even when you can't see where it's going.

The path ahead remained uncertain. My questions were still unanswered. But for the first time in a long time, I wasn't afraid of the dark.

Because I knew I wasn't walking through it alone.

CHAPTER 24

The Crucible Chronicles

I OPENED A FRESH NOTE ON MY phone and titled it *The Crucible Chronicles*. That note became a living document, my place to tell the truth in real time. Writing in it became a daily practice. The Crucible Chronicles kept the edges of my awareness sharp and my eye for miracles elevated. It was a way for me to stay present to whatever was unfolding, even when parts of me wanted to check out or disappear. Because maybe, just maybe, I might tell this story one day.

Closing off my heart to harden it against the ache would have been easier. But my deeper intention became a question I carried like a compass: *How fully can I feel all of this, and how quickly can I let it go?*

I wanted to stay awake to life, even when that meant watching the unraveling. To be the witness and the participant all at once, I knew, began with honesty.

Around that time, I was invited to speak at a mastermind event to a room full of founders, investors, and high-performing operators. My instinct was to perform—to put on the armor, present the highlight reel, say what you're supposed to say when people ask how things are going. But as I took the stage that day, that familiar whisper insisted on one thing.

Tell the truth.

So I shared the heartbreak, the fear, the slow, aching unraveling of something I loved. I told them what it looked like to be in the middle of the fire, not on the other side of it. To my surprise, the energy in the room didn't shrink. It opened. People leaned in and nodded along. I even saw some wiping tears.

People approached me afterward to tell me their own stories of failed launches, near-breakdowns, parts of their stories they'd been carrying in silence. What connected us wasn't the illusion of strength. It was the shared language of being human. Because without exception, we are all facing challenges. And the thing we are most likely to have in common is usually the last thing that we want to talk about.

I had shared stories from my scars before, but never from inside the healing process. That day, I spoke not as a hero who slayed his dragon, but as someone still facing the flames, the disappointment, and uncertainty about what came next. There is something special that happens when we're willing to speak from the middle of the mess, instead of pretending we're already through it.

I made a silent commitment to carry this honesty and presence throughout this period of my life. When people asked how I was feeling during that time, I said, "I'm feeling!" If they asked, "How is life?" I said, "Life is life-ing!"

The next morning, Rob and I met to begin mapping the path forward. We named four priorities. First, our team—we would give them as much notice, clarity, and care as possible. Second, our customers—we would find a way for them to receive ongoing support, even if we couldn't offer it ourselves. Third, our investors—we owed them a final attempt to recover whatever we could to honor their trust in us. And lastly, ourselves—to reduce our personal liability, which could add up to hundreds of thousands of dollars. That reality hovered in the background of everything, but we had to put it aside and do what was best for the business.

There was no map for what we were navigating, only our shared commitment to move through it in a way we could be proud of and would let us sleep well at night. We would close this chapter with as much integrity as we had brought to building it. Thankfully, we had Dad, who had navigated similar scenarios one too many times in his career. He offered both practical guidance for us and an inspiration that we, too, could make it to the other side.

The hardest part came first: telling the team. They had seen the signs, but hearing it out loud hit differently. We met in The Summit Room. The space that had held excitement, launches, late-night sessions, and birthday cakes now held the gravity of an ending. The room fell still and reverent. Cat sat wide-eyed, stunned, yet ready to help. Chad's loyalty burned bright. "I'd bet my entire salary on an ad campaign," he said without flinching. TJ was empathetic and supportive. Curt and Pat offered to cut their contracts in half. Jake pulled me aside after our meeting, voice catching, and said he felt he'd received more than he gave. Doug, though clearly burnt out, remained steady and kept showing up to lay bricks until the very end. Jack, our warehouse manager, shed tears not for himself but for what we must be going through.

What came back to us was loyalty through the finish. The team's kindness and support humbled me. The way they carried the load with us, even in the end, said everything.

Eighty tubs remained in the warehouse, and we needed to sell them all to settle the business debt and fund our wind-down operations. But we couldn't, in good conscience, sell them for full price knowing we wouldn't be around to honor the warranties. That was a hard line both Rob and I agreed on, though it made our jobs more difficult. So we cut the price by more than half and launched a clear inventory blowout sale, which required each buyer to check a box, consenting to no warranty on their purchase. To our relief, the orders still poured in.

On the morning of October 31, 2024, the day we were announcing the closure, I woke up differently than I expected. Instead of sinking into the heaviness, I felt a pulse of energy. I got out of bed, hit the gym, got into the cold plunge, did my breathwork, and built my state from the inside out. I made a clear decision: today, I would be the thermostat, not the thermometer. I would set the temperature, not react to it.

My team needed me to show up at that level. I needed myself to show up at that level. And so I did. It felt like a small graduation, a marker of growth I didn't even know I was working toward. On the toughest day of my business career so far, I chose to show up with energy and presence. I showed up for myself first. That inner resilience—the ability to choose our state in the middle of a storm—might be the most important skill we can build as humans and certainly as entrepreneurs.

When it came time to share the news with our community, the emotions came in a full spectrum. Sadness, grief, fear, anxiety. But also relief. And even joy. Beneath all of it was a steady current of gratitude. It surprised me how strong it was. Gratitude for the whole ride. Gratitude for how beautiful the journey had been. Gratitude for each person who played a role in it.

It hurt because it mattered. And maybe that was the point. To feel the full spectrum. To go all in. To find the edges of our emotional and energetic capacity. To build the strength to meet whatever comes next with an open heart and a grounded state.

Character is revealed in challenge. I had learned that years earlier, battling back from surgery after surgery. Adversity doesn't define you; it merely gives you the chance to define yourself. After all, a calm sea never made a skilled sailor.

Before stepping out of my car that morning, I pulled out my phone and opened The Crucible Chronicles. I typed a quick note with what was present: *Thank you, God, for the opportunity to define myself. For the chance to rise. To show who I really am. Thank you for these gifts. I see them already.*

We gathered in the conference room one last time. Rob sat to my right, where he always sat. Cat sat on my left, Chad beside her. Nikita joined from Portugal, his face pixilated on the screen, but his heart was fully present with us. We took a deep breath and put the finishing touches on the email no founder ever wants to write.

The subject line said it all: *Edge Theory Labs Has Gone Out of Business.*

Rob and I had spent hours crafting the letter that would go out to our customers and more than 70,000 Instagram followers:

Dear Edge Theory Labs Community,

It is with a heavy heart that we share some difficult news: Edge Theory Labs is closing its doors.

This message is one we never thought we'd have to write, and it's hard to put into words the sense of loss we feel and regret that we will not be able to serve our community and customers moving forward.

Edge Theory Labs started as a passion project between two cousins—a simple attempt to upgrade our chest freezer and to continue to get the most out of the life-changing benefits we experienced from the practice of cold water immersion. From those early days tinkering in the garage, we could never have imagined the impact our work would have. Watching so many of you go all in, challenge your limits, and share your stories has been a true honor. It's something we will always hold close to our hearts.

Despite our best efforts to keep Edge Theory Labs moving forward, we faced critical challenges that we simply could not overcome. As cold water immersion has taught us, we chose to embrace the challenges head-on with everything that we have.

Over the past year, we faced complex manufacturing challenges that made it difficult to uphold the high-quality standards we envisioned. Addressing these issues required resources that, amid a rapidly shifting market and declining sales, proved beyond reach. This is a struggle we've seen impact other companies in our industry, forcing some to close their doors as well.

We've poured everything we have—and then some—into finding a way to make it work. But sometimes life doesn't work out the way you plan, despite your best efforts, honest intention

We know this is disappointing and will cause frustration and challenges for many of you, and we are deeply sorry. It breaks our hearts that we can no longer provide the post-purchase support that we committed to.

Throughout this journey, we've operated with a commitment to putting our customers first, and though we're closing our doors, we're doing everything possible to leave you in good hands with resources and options to support you moving forward. More information on this can be found on our website.

Thank you for every step you took with us, for every testimonial and story you shared, and for being part of Edge Theory Labs. This community has made this journey so rewarding, and we're honored to have been a part of your lives.

With deep appreciation and our sincerest apologies,
Rob and Joshua Church

That moment in the conference room felt surreal. It felt like how I imagine the losing team must feel after the Super

Bowl—after months of building, training, and pushing beyond every limit—when the final whistle blows and all that's left is to face the loss after coming so close.

And just like that, with a simple click, it was sent. No one moved or spoke. Eyes stared past laptops and empty coffee mugs, absorbing the reality of the moment.

A few days earlier, Rob and I had called the investors, partners, and athletes who had backed us to share the news first. But now that the news was public, the ripple effect happened. Instagram lit up. Texts came pouring in. Friends, customers, distant connections, all asking the same question: "What happened?" Their words came with genuine confusion. From the outside, we appeared to be thriving. But there had been a disconnect during the last year between what people saw and what was actually happening behind the curtain. The truth never fit cleanly into a square frame or highlight reel.

Those final days were messy, not in a disorganized sense, but in the human sense. There was emotion everywhere. Joy tangled with Grief. Peace bumping against Panic. Gratitude threaded through every hard goodbye. Rob and I handled each task with the same care we'd used to glue every single valve to those first tubs.

One by one, the action items that had overwhelmed us began to shrink. We cleared our inventory. We found a way to negotiate a resolution with our secured creditor, who met our honesty with understanding. Even our landlord released us from the office lease. Bit by bit, we cleaned up the pieces of what was once our whole world.

By the end of November, the office was hollow. The enthusiastic buzz of creation had gone quiet. There were no more Slack pings or laughter from the marketing corner. Amidst the echoes of those sounds were just two founders cleaning up the remains of their dreams. Rob and I disassembled the furniture we had once built together. We cleared shelves, pulled up flooring, and boxed up the items left to sell. It was strange, but it felt sacred in its own way.

Most of our final conversations went better than expected. Nine times out of ten, we were met with grace. Investors thanked us for our honesty. Partners listened with understanding. Customers responded with kindness. Each exchange gave me just enough breath to keep going.

But there was one out of ten that cut deep.

An email landed in my inbox with a subject line that made my chest tighten before I even opened it.

You're a fraud.

I hesitated. Then clicked.

The message was short, but sharp enough to draw blood.

You are a fraud. Professing 'all eyes on God.' You ask Him to bless you with the ability to defraud people, you spineless weasel. It's people like you that give God a bad name. Be a man and give people their money back. I will personally make sure that any endeavor you try and get into, your audience will know the character of who they are dealing with. Sent from my iPhone.

I sat there, rereading it, the words sinking down past my skin. My hands twitched with the urge to respond. I wanted to explain. To lay it all out. To show the sender all the sleepless nights, the impossible choices, the sacrifices we poured into trying to save the business. I imagined writing something so honest and detailed that he'd have no choice but to see me differently.

But even as I played out the response in my mind, I knew it would be wasted. He wasn't writing to understand. He was writing to wound. Because he was wounded.

I forwarded the email to Giorgio. I needed to hear someone else's voice. He sent back a voice note, calm and steady.

"Don't bother," he said. "Think about the energy it would take to try to change this man's mind. You probably won't succeed. And even if you did—what would it give you? Look to the people who know you. The ones who've walked with you through the fire. That's what matters."

He was right. I closed my laptop and let the ache pass through me. The pain had something to teach me. That email, brutal as it was, had become a mirror and a test for me. And as I got quiet again, I heard a new phrase whispered: *New level, new devil.*

You don't move to the next stage of anything without facing the boss. That's how the game is played. That's how the soul is forged. Maybe, this man, this message, this moment was the final boss before whatever came next. Because when I really looked at how the Edge story unfolded, this season of unraveling had given me something priceless. It had forced me into a depth I might never have reached any other way. And more than anything, it brought me closer to God. It showed me that God is, in fact, the rock at the rock bottom. Somehow, even in the wreckage, I could feel Him there—steady beneath the shifting ground, preparing me for what was yet to come as he always has.

The Universe, in its unmistakable way, restored balance to the equation. The next day, Dana White called. His tone was warm, curious, and unexpectedly tender. He asked what had happened, how he could offer support, and reminded me that even in loss, there is always something to be gained.

Rob and I held onto one last piece of office equipment longer than we probably should have. Even after the conference room table was gone, the sauna remained. It had always been our space for reflection, a place where the steam softened the edges of hard conversations. Its wood walls had absorbed years of clarity, frustration, big dreams, and silent prayers.

Now, with the sale of the sauna finalized for the next day, Rob and I entered it for one final sweat. The heat pressed in around us in its familiar density, the air full of memory. Rob sat across from me, his shoulders slumped, face damp with sweat, eyes dark and tired.

After a long silence, his voice cracked through the stillness.

"I'm sorry, bro," he said. "I wish I could've done more. We were so close."

I nodded, the grief sitting between us like an unwelcome yet inevitable third wheel.

"I know, brother," I said. "It's not your fault, though. We gave it our all."

I closed my eyes and let it all rise—the sweat along my spine, the ache in my heart, the sticky grief of *what could have been*. And beneath it all, something softer settled. A quiet peace that had been growing slowly during the previous few weeks. A whisper clear as day: *What if you didn't fail?*

From one view, yes—we objectively failed. The business closed. The mission, at least in its original form, ended. But from another view, the one that feels truer now, we didn't lose. We built something people cared about. Something that positively impacted the lives of tens of thousands of people. We built a team that loved each other. We learned lessons no classroom could have taught and met people who would stay with us far beyond this chapter. We gave everything we had. We stepped into the arena knowing it could break our hearts—and we showed up anyway. We took the shot. We found our Edge.

That feels like one heck of a win to me.

The sauna falls silent again to the soft hiss of steam on stone and the steady drip of sweat on cedar. Rob leans back, eyes closed, head resting against the wood. I watch him for a moment—my brother in arms—and feel the unmistakable thrum of gratitude. Not only had we built something real, we had let it go with love, with honor, and with integrity.

There was beauty in that, maybe even something holy.

By Thanksgiving, most of the team had stepped into new positions elsewhere. The machine of the world kept turning, as it always does. Without an income and having just poured my savings into this business, I had to move out of my apartment. Thankfully, I had the chance to move back home to my parents' house, even if it was just a mattress on the floor of my brother's room.

But even then, I didn't feel lost. I didn't feel like I had failed. I felt surprisingly steady, which surprised me. My worst-case scenario had arrived, and I was still here. Still breathing, still intact. The world had not collapsed. In fact, I felt lighter.

I leaned into the few things that brought me back to myself—breathwork, prayer, cold plunges, quiet walks, long conversations with friends who saw me without needing an explanation. I leaned into God, into community, and into the mystery of not knowing what happens next. I held on to the belief that this *is* the fun, you see. I had been here before.

In that mystery, a new kind of clarity began to rise. On the trail of following cosmic breadcrumbs, one of those breadcrumbs I picked up was the very thing I feared the most. But what if God led me there not to punish me, but to free me?

Maybe it's his way of showing me that I never had anything to fear all along.

CHAPTER 25

The Next Breadcrumb

The Universe, fittingly, closed the chapter on Edge Theory Labs not with punctuation, but with poetry.

In early December, a few weeks before handing the keys over to our landlord and finishing the wind-down, I showed up for one final commitment. Months earlier—before we knew how the story would end—I had agreed to set up a tub at a wellness event in San Diego. We'd canceled everything else, but this one stayed on the calendar because it came through a close friend. I felt it was only right to see that commitment through, even though we were out of business.

That morning, I woke up groggy and tender, scanning my inbox for the event details. I vaguely remembered that the event was taking place downtown. And then I saw the location.

The Guild Hotel San Diego.

I said it aloud and let out a half-laugh, half-sob. My eyes filled with tears before I could stop them.

The Guild Hotel was where we met our first customer three years earlier. It was where Zander and I led our big workshop the same week Rob, Cat, and I launched Edge Theory Labs.

And now, somehow, it was coming full circle. The same space that witnessed the birth of an idea would now memorialize its closing chapter. That very courtyard I set up our prototype tub for the first time which brought us our first sale would be the scene for the last Edge Tub setup I would do.

I cried the entire drive there. Not from sadness alone, but from a release as if I crashed into a hug and my whole nervous system could finally exhale.

One more time, I wheeled the chiller through the polished lobby and out to the sun-drenched patio. Being there felt like deja vu. The beginning and the end, mirroring each other like reflections in still water.

On New Year's Eve, Rob and I met at the warehouse one last time to remove our final load of gear and hand over the keys to our landlord. Just one brand-new tub remained; everything else was gone.

While we waited for our landlord to arrive, we noticed a new tenant moving into the space next door. I recognized him immediately: a friend of Zander's I'd met a few times over the years. We struck up a casual conversation, and a few minutes later, his cofounder joined us. When we told him what we were doing, he lit up. He said that he'd been following Edge for a while and mentioned how bummed he was to have missed our inventory blowout sale.

Rob and I exchanged a glance and smiled. Ten minutes later, we were loading our last Edge Tub into his trunk, which he bought with cash on the spot.

Even our final sale carried its own kind of grace.

Another thread. Another loop closed. As if the Universe wasn't merely wrapping things up, but rather—it was writing a love letter. A quiet reminder that we were still being held.

After handing the keys to the landlord, Rob and I walked to the brewery down the street and sat down. The air was cool with winter sun shining, and the smell of hops calmed me instantly. For the first time in weeks, we didn't have any tough conversations or decisions ahead of us. We could let ourselves be still.

"Man," Rob said, taking a sip, "we really did the damn thing, huh?"

I nodded, my throat thick with everything we'd just lived through. "Yeah. We sure did."

He raised his glass. "An honor and a privilege."

I clinked mine against his. "An honor and a privilege."

Edge Theory Labs was no longer something we were building. It was something we had built. A story complete.

After we parted ways, I didn't go straight home. I followed a quiet pull toward the beach.

I walk the familiar stretch where ocean meets land, the tide rolling in slowly and steadily to my right. Its rhythmic, eternal breath softens my edges, as it always does. To my left, the sandstone cliffs and reef of Carlsbad stand timeless and worn, their jagged lines weathered into grace much like my own. The sand is warm beneath my feet, giving just slightly with each step.

The late afternoon light paints everything in gold. Even the seagulls leisurely slow their pace at this tender hour. A breeze rolls off the water, carrying the unmistakable scent of salt and sun-baked kelp, and I feel the swirl of endings and beginnings intertwined in nature, just as they have in my own life.

I've walked this path through so many versions of myself, through doubt and devotion, through endings and breakthroughs. I don't have a destination in mind. Only a need to feel connected again—to life, to God, to whatever comes next. I move slowly, allowing my thoughts to rise and fall with the waves. A quiet smile finds its way to my face, not for any reason I can name, just the natural side effect of being fully *here*. For the first time in a long time, nothing feels urgent.

Then, as if summoned by the quiet of my mind, a small figure darts into my peripheral vision.

A little boy, maybe eight years old, comes sprinting toward me out of nowhere. He skids to a stop in front of me, beaming, his cheeks flushed with sun and joy, his nose streaked with white zinc.

"Look what I found!" he exclaims, holding out his closed fist with theatrical suspense. He opens his hand to reveal a small, wiggling sand crab, its tiny legs twitching against his palm like an orchestra warming up.

"Whoa," I breathe, caught completely off guard, not just by the crab, but by the spontaneous eruption of this connection. This boy looks at me as if we've always known each other. Somehow, it feels like maybe we have.

Before I can say anything else, he grabs my hand and tugs me toward the reef. He doesn't ask or check; he just leads me there as if he'd been planning all day for me to join him, and I was late but had finally arrived.

On the reef are two other kids, his siblings, I assume, since they're wearing matching suits and share a certain air of mischief in their body language. All three kids are within that bold and beautiful stage of childhood when curiosity overrules caution. They are hunched over the shallow tide pools, scouring the cracks and puddles for more sand crabs with the dedication of scientists but the freedom of wild things. Each time they find a crab, they place it gently into a separate tide pool they have claimed as their holding tank. The crabs can easily crawl out, and many do, which keeps the whole game going in an infinite loop of play.

I crouch down beside them, careful not to disrupt their rhythm. They are so focused on the task at hand that the brother and sister accept me without as much as looking up. I'm just part of the game now. Just another set of eyes on the lookout, another pair of hands to lift stones and point out treasures. One of them lets out an enthusiastic shout, "Big crab over here!" and we all scramble to admire it.

Some of these crabs are not small. I marvel at their bravery and ask, "Do they ever pinch you?"

"Yeah," the boy replies without looking up.

"Does it hurt?" I ask, more curious than concerned.

"Yeah," he says again, this time his eyes meet mine. "But that's okay. They just don't know we're trying to help them. It's for their own good."

The words linger in the salt air, reverberating deeper than he could ever know. Maybe this is how God handles me—patient and present, willing to let the pinch happen when it serves a greater purpose. A presence that doesn't insulate me from pain, but stays with me through it. A love that holds steady, even when I thrash against the hand that's trying to help.

We play like this for a while, maybe five minutes, maybe twenty. Time ceases to exist. At one point, I look at them and ask, "This is so much fun. Is this what you do all day?"

The young girl looks up for the first time, a glimmer of sass and spark in her voice. "No. We also boogie board, too."

Of course. How dare I forget about boogie boarding?

As gently as I arrived, I sense it's my moment to go. I stand up, brushing sand from my palms.

"Thanks for showing me your game," I say. "I'll see you guys around."

"Bye!" they chirp without looking back, already pulled into pursuit of the next crab.

I turn and continue south, laughing softly to myself as I walk. The sand stretches before me, rippling like golden fabric. I know this road. This path of cosmic breadcrumbs is the one I've been following all along. The voice that led me to the mirror that night when I felt close to death. The one who whispered to give Ohio one more shot. The one who told me to forget about the wine opener, and carried me to Iceland, and taught me how to heal at the deepest level. The one who brought me back into my body and taught me to listen to the language of intuition. The one that led me to discover my gifts, my passion, and my purpose.

Now, here it is again. I feel it unfolding beneath my feet, quiet and steady, lit by the late afternoon sun like it's always known the way, even if I don't.

So I keep walking. Barefoot. Still smiling. The laughter of the reef kids is still bouncing off the cliffs beside me. I don't know exactly what is next, but I trust it. I trust who I've become. I trust the foundation I've built—the habits, the perspective, the lessons etched into me like lines in stone. I trust my capacity to keep going. And I trust the presence walking with me. My Creator. My partner in the Universe.

I am surrendered to whatever is in my highest good. I know with all my heart and all my might that what is meant for me cannot miss me. I am ready to follow wherever the path leads.

I don't know where I'm going next, but I'm on my way.

All I need to do is follow the next cosmic breadcrumb.

I know it's already waiting for me, just ahead.

**For additional content and resources,
Please follow the QR code below.**